A   Beh

CW00531005

Heinemann
ASSEMBLY
Resources

THEMES &

READINGS

for

Assemblies

COMPILED BY

SUSANNA REID

Heinemann

Heinemann Educational Publishers
Halley Court, Jordan Hill, Oxford OX2 8EJ
a division of Reed Educational & Professional Publishing Ltd

OXFORD FLORENCE PRAGUE MADRID ATHENS
MELBOURNE AUCKLAND KUALA LUMPUR SINGAPORE
TOKYO IBADAN NAIROBI KAMPALA JOHANNESBURG
GABORONE PORTSMOUTH NH (USA) CHICAGO
MEXICO CITY SAO PAULO

To my husband, Donald

01 00 99 98 97 10 9 8 7 6 5 4 3 2 1

British Library Cataloguing in Publication Data

A catalogue record for this book is available from the British Library

ISBN 0 435 30251 5

Cover designed by Threefold Design
Designed and typeset by TechType, Abingdon, Oxon.
Printed and bound in Great Britain by Biddles Ltd, Guildford

Contents

◆

Acknowledgements

The publishers would like to thank the following for permission to reproduce copyright material:

The Bishop of Oxford, The Rt Reverend Richard Harries for the article 'Saint who loved one-liners' published in *The Times*, 31 July 1993, pp. 161–2; A & C Black (Publishers) Ltd. for an extract from *Albert Schweitzer: An Anthology*, edited by Charles R Joy, pp. 164–5; Cambridge University Press for verses from the *New English Bible*, © Oxford University Press and Cambridge University Press 1961, 1970, for verses and Psalm 104 from *The Authorized Version of the Bible* (The King James Bible), and for Psalm 150 from *The Book of Common Prayer*. The rights in *The Authorized Version of the Bible* (The King James Bible) and *The Book of Common Prayer* are vested in the Crown and are reproduced by permission of the Crown's Patentee, Cambridge University Press; Crease Harman and Co. on behalf of the estate of Bruce Hutchison for an extract from *The Far Side of the Street* by Bruce Hutchison, p. 153; Curtis Brown Group, London, for an extract from *The Wind in the Willows* by Kenneth Graham, © The University Chest, Oxford, pp. 140–42; Darton Longman & Todd Ltd. for an extract from *Good Friday People* by Sheila Cassidy (1991) p. 104 and for verses from *The New Jerusalem Bible* published 1985 with Doubleday & Co.; Faber and Faber Ltd. for an extract from a postcard from Sylvia Plath published in *Letters Home* by Sylvia Plath, pp. 139–140 and for the poems 'The Cultivation of Christmas Trees', p. 13, 'Journey of the Magi', pp. 15–16, two lines from 'Choruses from The Rock', p. 147 and ten lines from 'Ash Wednesday' from *Collected Poems 1909–1962* by TS Eliot; Gill & Macmillan for two poems from *Prayers of Life* by Michel Quoist, pp. 47–8 and 126–7; Victor Gollancz Ltd. for an extract from *One Day in the Life of Ivan Denisovitch* by Alexander Solzhenitsyn, translated by Ralph Parker, p. 107 and for extracts from *A Year of Grace* by Victor Gollancz, p. 132; Mrs Jacqueline Gryn for a quote by Rabbi Hugo Gryn, p. 107; HarperCollins Publishers for an extract from *The Door Wherein I Went* by Lord Hailsham, pp. 35–6, for the story *The Lion, the Witch and the Wardrobe* by C S Lewis, pp. 31–2 and 33–4, for an extract from *A Precocious Autobiography* by Yevgeny Yevtushenko on p. 115 and for verses from *The Bible* (Fount Paperbacks); A M Heath & Company Ltd. on behalf of the estate of the late Pierre d'Harcourt for an extract from *The Real Enemy is Within*, pp. 102–103; The Heirs to the Estate of Martin Luther King, Jr. for the copyright extract from Integrated Bus Suggestions by Martin Luther King, Jr., pp. 165–7; David Higham Associates Ltd. on behalf of Elizabeth Jennings for the poem 'Afterthought' from *The Poems* published by Carcanet Press Ltd., p. 11 and on behalf of Louis MacNeice for the poem 'Prayer before Birth' from *Collected Poems* published by Faber and Faber Ltd. pp. 100–101; Hodder & Stoughton Ltd. for the story 'Coping with Grandpa' from *Smoke on the Mountain* by Joy Davidman pp. 111–112 and for an extract from *Words of Worship* by Champling and Davis published by Edward Arnold Ltd., pp. 118–119; Methuen & Co. for an extract from *The Life of Blessed Henry Suso*, translated by T F Knox, p. 151; The Missionaries of Charity for extracts from *A Gift for God* by Mother Theresa, pp. 122 and 124–5, and an extract from *Something Beautiful for God* by Malcolm Muggeridge, pp. 54–6 and 168–9; Mowbray (Imprint of Cassell PLC) for three stories from *Acts of Worship for Assemblies* by R H Lloyd, pp. 4, 44–6 and 158 and a Prayer from *Services for Betweenagers* by R H Lloyd, p. 171; John Murray (Publishers) Ltd. for the poem 'The Conversion of St. Paul' by John Betjeman from his *Uncollected Poems* pp. 75–7 and for the poem 'Christmas' by John Betjeman from his *Collected Poems* pp. 6–7; National Council of the Churches of Christ in the USA for quotations from the *Revised Standard Version of the Bible*, © 1946, 1952, 1971 by the Division of Christian Education of the National Council of the Churches of Christ in the USA; Oxford University Press for a quote by Simone Weil, translated by Richard Rees from *Selected Essays* (1962), p. 121 and for an extract from *What I Believe* by Tolstoy (1921) translated by Aylmer Maude (The World's Classics) pp. 94–5; Penguin UK for an extract from *How Can We Know?* by A N Wilson, p. 162, for the story 'King Midas: The King with the Golden Touch' from *Metamorphosis of Ovid* by Mary Innes, pp. 107–8 and for an extract from Resurrection by Tolstoy translated by Rosemary Edmonds, p. 124; Mrs Vera Phillips for extracts from *The New Testament in Modern English* translated by J B Phillips (Collins Fount Paperbacks) published by HarperCollins Publishers; Reed Books for an extract from *The Brothers Karamazov* by Dostoevsky, translated by Constance Garnett, p. 150; Routledge Ltd. for a quotation from *Basic Verities* by Charles Peguy, translated by Ann and Julian Green, p. 121; The Royal Society for the Encouragement of Arts, Manufacture & Commerce for an extract from a lecture 'Giving a Childhood to our Children' by Daniel Miller, delivered to the Society 4 March 1992, and published in the RSA Journal, July 1992, p. 41; Richard Scott Simon Ltd. on behalf of the Joyce Grenfell Memorial Trust for a poem from *By Herself and Her Friends* published by Macmillan & Company. © Joyce and Reggie Grenfell 1990, p. 85; The Society of Authors as the literary representatives of the estate of James Stephens for the poem 'A Singing in the Air' from *Christmas at Freelands*. p. 6; The Society for Promoting Christian Knowledge for two extracts from *The Seven Storey Mountain* by Thomas Merton, pp. 154 and 156; A P Watt Ltd. on behalf of The National Trust for an extract from *Kim* by Rudyard Kipling, pp. 143–144, on behalf of the Literary Executors of the Estate of H G Wells for an extract from *The Outline of History*, p. 31 and on behalf of the Royal Literary Fund for the poem 'The Donkey' and 'Orthodoxy' by G K Chesterton, pp. 23 and 25.

The publishers have made every effort to contact the correct copyright holders. However, if any material has been incorrectly acknowledged, we will be pleased to correct this at the earliest opportunity.

Introduction

♦

Themes and Readings for Assemblies is designed for use in secondary schools and the readings will appeal particularly to pupils over 14. Older pupils could be encouraged to perform the readings and it tends to work best if two of them do it together.

Most of the readings in this book come from the Bible and are included to help pass on a knowledge of the Bible to students. In the majority of cases The New English Bible has been used but in some instances other translations have been preferred. Full details on which translations have been used are given in Appendix 2.

Extracts have been chosen and arranged under themes in order to help teachers who organize school assemblies. Passages are divided into 'days' in which there may be one or more readings. In some cases a biblical reading will stand better on its own; in other cases it is accompanied by one from another source to illustrate or complement it.

The length of the passages inevitably varies. In an assembly when there are extensive notices or musical performances, shorter passages could be used. For a longer assembly, or service, groups of several readings on one subject could be used together, and the division into days altered according to the time available.

Sections 1–7 follow the story of Christ and his Church. These sections could be read as a story over a period of time or, if preferred, parts could be selected as appropriate for the time of year. Sections 8 and 9 provide readings which are sources of moral teaching and which are sufficiently varied to work as a sequence. Chapter 9, on the Ten Commandments, can be presented as an example of rules of life which have formed the basis of both moral and criminal codes for thousands of years. Sections 10 and 11 are about religious experience and they could be used alternately with other readings or, in the case of Section 11, as a source of readings for special occasions such as Harvest Festivals, the beginnings and ends of terms, or school celebrations. Section 12, about saints and saintly people, makes an interesting sequence and could be supplemented with other readings such as the one about Oscar Romero in Section 8. This could provide a starting point for pupils to contribute their own ideas about people whom they admire and who come into this category.

The contents list enables the user to see at a glance how the readings are grouped. However, the index provides a list which may be useful if a particular subject is topical either on the news or in the school, and if the book is being used simply as a source of occasional readings. For Remembrance Day, for example, there are passages about war and our attitude to enemies.

Some prayers have also been included, in Appendix 1. For each, suggestions are given as to when they might best be used with the readings.

These readings will be useful in Church schools but in most schools they are not intended to provide a complete assembly book as readings about other faiths must also be used. Pupils need knowledge about religions if they are to be in a position to make a free choice about their beliefs as they grow up. This will enable them to develop their own spirituality and help them to understand the connection between this and moral ideas.

In her 'Manifesto for the Nation', Frances Lawrence, the widow of the murdered headmaster Philip Lawrence, says that the 'abiding values' of religion are 'of paramount importance' and 'one leading principle of this document.' She continues: 'Representatives of all faiths will be vital members of future debate.' Anyone who is part of this debate, about the threat of moral anarchy in our society, and who sees life as a spiritual pilgrimage will find some enlightenment in these readings.

Thanks

I am grateful to Barbara Webb for giving me a chance to use these readings in school; to Jackie Anderson for suggesting that they should be published; to my family for their patience and encouragement; to Janet Stevens for typing the text; and to Sue Walton for her editorial help.

1

Readings for Christmas

These readings are designed for assemblies towards the end of the Autumn Term. The final ones (Day 5) are Epiphany readings that could be used either then or at the beginning of the Spring Term.

Day 1

In the prophetic books of the Old Testament, a picture emerges of an ideal ruler longed for by the people of Israel. They assumed that he would be descended from their greatest King, David, whose father was called Jesse.

We too can share in this longing for a leader who could live up to such an ideal.

Isaiah, chapter 11, verses 1–5

Then a shoot shall grow from the stock of Jesse,
and a branch shall spring from his roots.
The spirit of the Lord shall rest upon him,
a spirit of wisdom and understanding,
a spirit of counsel and power,
a spirit of knowledge and the fear of the Lord.
He shall not judge by what he sees
nor decide by what he hears;
he shall judge the poor with justice
and defend the humble in the land with equity;
his mouth shall be a rod to strike down the ruthless,
and with a word he shall slay the wicked.
Round his waist he shall wear the belt of justice,
and good faith shall be the girdle round his body.

*This next reading is also about a ruler, a Russian prince. Through the
prince's story, the writer has attempted to find some equivalent to the
way in which God came to earth at Christmas.*

The story of the Russian prince
by R H Lloyd

Long ago in nineteenth-century Russia the young Prince Demetrie
inherited a large estate and great riches from his father. Unlike many
of the wealthy landowners who lived in Russia at that time, Prince
Demetrie was passionately interested in the welfare of the poor people who worked on his land and who lived in terrible poverty and
squalor. He constantly visited their villages and homes and tried to
show them how they could improve things, but to no avail. They lis-
tened respectfully of course and agreed with what he had to say, but
did nothing about it. To them he was someone who lived in another
world! How could he possibly know what it was like to live in their
conditions? How could he ever understand? Prince Demetrie was not
slow to realize why he wasn't getting across to them, and decided to
change his tactics.

A few years later, a bearded man dressed in threadbare and
patched clothing turned up in one of the villages and rented a small
room from one of the inhabitants. He said he was a doctor, and was
immediately besieged with patients who had never met a doctor
before. All sorts of medicines and pills were handed out and lots of
advice given about hygiene and diet. Soon everything began to
improve, and the doctor moved on to the next village and the next,
renting a room here and there, always available and always ready to
help.

All the people on Prince Demetrie's estate benefited from the
teaching and good works of the doctor. The streets were swept,
drains were dug, homes were kept spotless and the daily diet was
carefully watched. A complete transformation took place in the lives
of all. And then the secret leaked out: the good doctor was none
other than Prince Demetrie. He knew that he would only truly reach
his people by totally identifying himself with them.

Day 2

The mystery of Christ's coming, heralded by John the Baptist, is expressed in the poetic language of the opening of St John's Gospel. 'The Word' in this passage suggests that, just as a person's thoughts are revealed in their words, so the thoughts of God are revealed in his creation and then in the life of his Son, Jesus Christ.

St John's Gospel, chapter 1, verses 1–18

In the beginning was the Word, and the Word was with God, and the Word was God. He was in the beginning with God; all things were made through him, and without him was not anything made that was made. In him was life, and the life was the light of men. The light shines in the darkness, and the darkness has not overcome it.

There was a man sent from God, whose name was John. He came for testimony, to bear witness to the light, that all might believe through him. He was not the light, but came to bear witness to the light.

The true light that enlightens every man was coming into the world. He was in the world, and the world was made through him, yet the world knew him not. He came to his own home, and his own people received him not. But to all who received him, who believed in his name, he gave power to become children of God; who were born, not of blood nor of the will of the flesh nor of the will of man, but of God.

And the Word became flesh and dwelt among us, full of grace and truth; we have beheld his glory, glory as of the only Son from the Father. (John bore witness to him and cried, 'This was he of whom I said, "He who comes after me ranks before me, for he was before me."') And from his fullness have we all received, grace upon grace. For the law was given through Moses; grace and truth came through Jesus Christ. No one has ever seen God; the only son, who is in the bosom of the Father, he has made him known.

♦

The mystery of Christmas is also expressed in this poem.

'A Singing in the Air'
by James Stephens

A snowy field! A stable piled
With straw! A donkey's sleepy pow!
A Mother beaming on a Child!
A Manger, and a munching cow!
These we all remember now
And airy voices, heard afar!
And three Magicians, and a Star!

Two thousand times of snow declare
That on the Christmas of the year
There is a singing in the air;
And all who listen for it hear
A fairy chime, a seraph strain,
Telling He is born again,
That all we love is born again.

John Betjeman writes in his poem about what Christmas means to us.

'Christmas'
by John Betjeman

The bells of waiting Advent ring,
The Tortoise stove is lit again
And lamp-oil light across the night
Has caught the streaks of winter rain
In many a stained-glass window sheen
From Crimson Lake to Hooker's Green.

The holly in the windy hedge
And round the Manor House the yew
Will soon be stripped to deck the ledge,
The altar, font and arch and pew,
So that the villagers can say
'The church looks nice' on Christmas Day.

Provincial public houses blaze
And Corporation tramcars clang,

On lighted tenements I gaze
Where paper decorations hang,
And bunting in the red Town Hall
Says 'Merry Christmas to you all.'

And London shops on Christmas Eve
Are strung with silver bells and flowers
As hurrying clerks the City leave
To pigeon-haunted classic towers,
And marbled clouds go scudding by
To many-steepled London sky.

And girls in slacks remember Dad,
And oafish louts remember Mum,
And sleepless children's hearts are glad,
And Christmas-morning bells say 'Come!'
Even to shining ones who dwell
Safe in the Dorchester Hotel.

And is it true? And is it true,
This most tremendous tale of all,
Seen in a stained-glass window's hue,
A Baby in an ox's stall?
The Maker of the stars and sea
Become a Child on earth for me?

And is it true? For if it is,
No loving fingers tying strings
Around those tissued fripperies,
The sweet and silly Christmas things,
Bath salts and inexpensive scent
And hideous tie so kindly meant,

No love that in a family dwells,
No carolling in frosty air,
Nor all the steeple-shaking bells
Can with this single Truth compare –
That God was Man in Palestine
And lives today in Bread and Wine.

Day 3

The following reading tells the story of Christmas.

St Luke's Gospel, chapter 2, verses 1–19

In those days a decree was issued by the Emperor Augustus for a registration to be made throughout the Roman world. This was the first registration of its kind; it took place when Quirinius was governor of Syria. For this purpose everyone made his way to his own town; and so Joseph went up to Judaea from the town of Nazareth in Galilee to register at the city of David, called Bethlehem, because he was of the house of David by descent; and with him went Mary who was betrothed to him. She was expecting a child, and while they were there the time came for her baby to be born, and she gave birth to a son, her first-born. She wrapped him in his swaddling clothes, and laid him in a manger, because there was no room for them to lodge in the house.

Now in this same district there were shepherds out in the fields, keeping watch through the night over their flock, when suddenly there stood before them an angel of the Lord, and the splendour of the Lord shone round them. They were terror-stricken, but the angel said, 'Do not be afraid; I have good news for you: there is great joy coming to the whole people. Today in the city of David a deliverer has been born to you – the Messiah, the Lord. And this is your sign: you will find a baby lying wrapped in his swaddling clothes, in a manger.' All at once there was with the angel a great company of the heavenly host, singing the praises of God:

'Glory to God in highest heaven,
and on earth his peace for men on whom his favour rests.'

After the angels had left them and gone into heaven the shepherds said to one another, 'Come, we must go straight to Bethlehem and see this thing that has happened, which the Lord has made known to us.' So they went with all speed and found their way to Mary and Joseph; and the baby was lying in the manger. When they saw him, they recounted what they had been told about this child; and all who heard were astonished at what the shepherds said. But Mary treasured up all these things and pondered over them. Meanwhile the shepherds returned glorifying and praising God for what they had heard and seen; it had all happened as they had been told.

◆

The writer in this next poem contrasts the coming of a king of the world with the coming of the King of Heaven.

'Preparations'
(Anonymous, sixteenth century)

Yet if His Majesty, our sovereign Lord,
Should of his own accord
Friendly himself invite,
And say 'I'll be your guest tomorrow night,'
How we should stir ourselves, call and command
All hands to work! 'Let no man idle stand!'

'Set me fine Spanish tables in the hall;
See they be fitted all;
Let there be room to eat
And order taken that there want no meat.
See every sconce and candlestick made bright,
That without tapers they may give a light.

'Look to the presence: are the carpets spread,
The dazie[1] o'er the head,
The cushions in the chairs,
And all the candles lighted on the stairs?
Perfume the chambers, and in any case
Let each man give attendance in his place!'

Thus, if a king were coming, would we do;
And 'twere good reason too;
For 'tis a duteous thing
To show all honour to an earthly king,
And after all our travail and our cost,
So he be pleased, to think no labour lost.

But at the coming of the King of Heaven
All's set at six and seven;
We wallow in our sin,
Christ cannot find a chamber in the inn.
We entertain Him always like a stranger,
And, as at first, still lodge Him in the manger.

[1]dazie: canopy

Robert Southwell, in this poem, raises the question of what is really of value in life.

'New Prince, New Pomp'
by Robert Southwell

Behold a silly tender babe
In freezing winter night
In homely manger trembling lies:
Alas! a piteous sight.

The inns are full; no man will yield
This little pilgrim bed;
But forced he is with silly beasts
In crib to shroud his head.

Despise not him for lying there;
First what he is inquire:
An orient pearl is often found
In depth of dirty mire.

Weigh not his crib, his wooden dish,
Nor beasts that by him feed;
Weigh not his mother's poor attire,
Nor Joseph's single weed.

This stable is a Prince's court,
This crib his chair of state,
The beasts are parcel of his pomp,
The wooden dish his plate.

The persons in that poor attire
His royal liveries wear;
The Prince himself is come from heaven.
This pomp is prized there.

With joy approach, O Christian wight,
Do homage to thy King;
And highly praise this humble pomp
Which he from heaven doth bring.

In this poem, Elizabeth Jennings shows how disappointing Christmas can be unless we hear its true message.

'Afterthought'
by Elizabeth Jennings

For weeks before it comes I feel excited, yet when it
At last arrives, things all go wrong:
My thoughts don't seem to fit.

I've planned what I'll give everyone and what they'll give to me,
And then on Christmas morning all
The presents seem to be

Useless and tarnished. I have dreamt that everything would come
To life – presents and people too.
Instead of that, I'm dumb,

And people say, 'How horrid! What a sulky little boy!'
And they are right. I can't seem pleased.
The lovely shining toy

I wanted so much when I saw it in a magazine
Seems pointless now. And Christmas too
No longer seems to mean

The hush, the star, the baby, people being kind again.
The bells are rung, sledges are drawn,
And peace on earth for men.

Day 4

This passage describes Christ's humble coming to this world and the suffering he endured.

St Paul's Letter to the Philippians, chapter 2, verses 5–11

Let your bearing towards one another arise out of your life in Christ Jesus. For the divine nature was his from the first; yet he did not think to snatch at equality with God, but made himself nothing, assuming the nature of a slave. Bearing the human likeness, revealed in human shape, he humbled himself, and in obedience accepted even death – death on a cross. Therefore God raised him to the heights and bestowed on him the name above all names, that at the name of Jesus every knee should bow – in heaven, on earth, and in the depths – and every tongue confess, 'Jesus Christ is Lord', to the glory of God the Father.

♦

The poet Robert Southwell also refers to the suffering which Christ had to undergo in order to establish the real meaning of the love, justice and mercy which Christians believe he brought into the world.

'The Burning Babe'
by Robert Southwell

As I in hoary winter's night
Stood shivering in the snow,
Surpris'd I was with sudden heat,
Which made my heart to glow;

And, lifting up a fearful eye
To view what fire was near,
A pretty Babe all burning bright
Did in the air appear;

Who, scorched with excessive heat,
Such floods of tears did shed
As though his floods should quench his flames,
Which with his tears were fed.

'Alas' (quoth he) 'but newly born,
In fiery heats I fry,
Yet none approach to warm their hearts,
Or feel my fire, but I.

My faultless breast the furnace is;
The fuel, wounding thorns;
Love is the fire, and sighs the smoke,
The ashes, shame and scorns.

The fuel Justice layeth on,
And Mercy blows the coals,
The metal in this furnace wrought
Are men's defiled souls;

For which, as now on fire I am
To work them to their good,
so will I melt into a bath
To wash them in my blood.'

With this he vanished out of sight,
And swiftly shrunk away,
And straight I called unto mind
That it was Christmas Day.

♦

T S Eliot looks at modern attitudes to Christmas, taking delight in the real wonder of a child and in the more adult awareness of the demands which Christianity makes on its followers.

'The Cultivation of Christmas Trees'
by T S Eliot

There are several attitudes towards Christmas,
Some of which we may disregard:
The social, the torpid, the patently commercial,
The rowdy (the pubs being open till midnight),
And the childish – which is not that of the child
For whom the candle is a star, and the gilded angel
Spreading its wings at the summit of the tree
Is not only a decoration, but an angel.
The child wonders at the Christmas Tree:
Let him continue in the spirit of wonder
At the Feast of an event not accepted as a pretext;
So that the glittering rapture, the amazement
Of the first-remembered Christmas Tree,
So that the surprises, delight in new possessions
(Each one with its peculiar and exciting smell),
The expectation of the goose or the turkey
And the expected awe on its appearance,
So that the reverence and the gaiety
May not be forgotten in later experience,
In the bored habituation, the fatigue, the tedium,
The awareness of death, the consciousness of failure,

Or in the piety of the convert
Which may be tainted with a self-conceit
Displeasing to God and disrespectful to the children
(And here I remember also with gratitude
St Lucy, her carol and her crown of fire):
So that before the end, the eightieth Christmas
(By 'eightieth' meaning whichever is the last)
The accumulated memories of annual emotion
May be concentrated into a great joy
Which shall be also a great fear, as on the occasion
When fear came upon every soul:
Because the beginning shall remind us of the end
And the first coming of the second coming.

Day 5

This passage tells the story of the coming of the kings.

St Matthew's Gospel, chapter 2, verses 1–12

Jesus was born at Bethlehem in Judaea during the reign of Herod. After his birth astrologers from the east arrived in Jerusalem, asking, 'Where is the child who is born to be king of the Jews? We observed the rising of his star, and we have come to pay him homage.' King Herod was greatly perturbed when he heard this; and so was the whole of Jerusalem. He called a meeting of the chief priests and lawyers of the Jewish people, and put before them the question: 'Where is it that the Messiah is to be born?' 'At Bethlehem in Judaea,' they replied; and they referred him to the prophecy which reads: 'Bethlehem in the land of Judah, you are far from least in the eyes of the rulers of Judah; for out of you shall come a leader to be the shepherd of my people Israel.'

Herod next called the astrologers to meet him in private, and ascertained from them the time when the star had appeared. He then sent them on to Bethlehem, and said, 'Go and make a careful inquiry for the child. When you have found him, report to me, so that I may go myself and pay him homage.'

They set out at the king's bidding; and the star which they had seen at its rising went ahead of them until it stopped above the place where the child lay. At the sight of the star they were overjoyed. Entering the house, they saw the child with Mary his mother, and bowed to the ground in homage to him; then they opened their treasures and offered him gifts: gold, frankincense, and myrrh. And being warned in a dream not to go back to Herod, they returned home another way.

♦

T S Eliot imagines the journey of the Magi, a search for the birth of a Saviour, which also led to an understanding of what that Saviour would suffer. The lives of the Magi too would be transformed.

'Journey of the Magi'
by T S Eliot

'A cold coming we had of it,
Just the worst time of the year
For a journey, and such a long journey:
The ways deep and the weather sharp,
The very dead of winter.'
And the camels galled, sore-footed, refractory,
Lying down in the melting snow.
There were times we regretted
The summer palaces on slopes, the terraces,
And the silken girls bringing sherbet.
Then the camel men cursing and grumbling
And running away, and wanting their liquor and women,
And the night-fires going out, and the lack of shelters,
and the cities hostile and the towns unfriendly
And the villages dirty and charging high prices:
A hard time we had of it.
At the end we preferred to travel at night,
Sleeping in snatches,
With the voices singing in our ears, saying
That this was all folly.

Then at dawn we came down to a temperate valley,
Wet, below the snow line, smelling of vegetation;

With a running stream and a water-mill beating the darkness,
And three trees on the low sky,
And an old white horse galloped away in the meadow.
Then we came to a tavern with vine-leaves over the lintel,
Six hands at an open door dicing for pieces of silver,
And feet kicking the empty wine-skins.
But there was no information, and so we continued
And arrived at evening, not a moment too soon
Finding the place: it was (you may say) satisfactory.

All this was a long time ago, I remember,
And I would do it again, but set down
This set down
This: were we led all that way for
Birth or Death? There was a Birth, certainly,
We had evidence and no doubt. I had seen birth and death,
But had thought they were different; this Birth was
Hard and bitter agony for us, like Death, our death.
We returned to our places, these Kingdoms,
But no longer at ease here, in the old dispensation,
With an alien people clutching their gods.
I should be glad of another death.

2

The life of Christ

◆

The story of the life of Christ could be read as a continuation of the previous chapter, during the Spring Term, leading up to Easter, although many passages, such as those about his character, would fit other occasions.

———◆———

Day 1

The life of Christ did not have a promising start. Having been born in a stable, he became, at a young age, a refugee. His parents fled with him to Egypt to escape the murderous tyranny of King Herod. Thus Christians believe Christ can be identified with all those who throughout the twentieth century have had to flee with only what they could carry, from wars and despotic rulers.

St Matthew's Gospel, chapter 2, verses 13–23

After they had gone, an angel of the Lord appeared to Joseph in a dream, and said to him, 'Rise up, take the child and his mother and escape with them to Egypt, and stay there until I tell you; for Herod is going to search for the child to do away with him.' So Joseph rose from sleep, and taking mother and child by night he went away with them to Egypt, and there he stayed till Herod's death. This was to fulfil what the Lord had declared through the prophet: 'I called my son out of Egypt.'

When Herod saw how the astrologers had tricked him he fell into a passion, and gave orders for the massacre of all children in Bethlehem and its neighbourhood, of the age of two years or less, corresponding with the time he had ascertained from the astrologers. So the words spoken through Jeremiah the prophet were fulfilled: 'A voice was heard in Rama, wailing and loud laments; it was Rachel weeping for her children, and refusing all consolation, because they were no more.'

The time came that Herod died; and an angel of the Lord appeared in a dream to Joseph in Egypt and said to him, 'Rise up, take the child and his mother, and go with them to the land of Israel, for the men who threatened the child's life are dead.' So he rose, took mother and child with him, and came to the land of Israel. Hearing, however, that Archelaus had succeeded his father Herod as king of Judaea, he was afraid to go there. And being warned by a dream, he withdrew to the region of Galilee; there he settled in a town called Nazareth. This was to fulfil the words spoken through the prophets: 'He shall be called a Nazarene.'

Day 2

There are few glimpses of the childhood of Christ in the Bible, but once, when his parents took him up to the Temple, he was recognized by an old man who foresaw that he would be the Messiah.

St Luke's Gospel, chapter 2, verses 25–35

Now there was a man in Jerusalem, whose name was Simeon, and this man was righteous and devout, looking for the consolation of Israel, and the Holy Spirit was upon him. And it had been revealed to him by the Holy Spirit that he should not see death before he had seen the Lord's Christ. And inspired by the Spirit he came into the temple; and when the parents brought in the child Jesus, to do for him according to the custom of the law, he took him up in his arms and blessed God and said: 'Lord, now lettest thou thy servant depart in peace, according to thy word; for mine eyes have seen thy salvation which thou hast prepared in the presence of all peoples, a light for revelation to the Gentiles and for glory to thy people Israel.'

And his father and his mother marvelled at what was said about him; and Simeon blessed them and said to Mary his mother: 'Behold, this child is set for the fall and rising of many in Israel, and for a sign that is spoken against, (and a sword will pierce through your own soul also) that thoughts out of many hearts may be revealed.'

◆

St John the Baptist also recognized that Jesus was the Messiah. He paved the way for Jesus by calling on people to repent and to change their way of life. He also told them about the greater man who was to follow. Here is a passage about St John.

St Luke's Gospel, chapter 3, verses 10–16

The people asked him, 'Then what are we to do?' He replied, 'The man with two shirts must share with him who has none, and anyone who has food must do the same.' Among those who came to be baptized were tax-gatherers, and they said to him, 'Master, what are we to do?' He told them, 'Exact no more than the assessment.' Soldiers on service also asked him, 'And what of us?' To them he said, 'No bullying; no blackmail; make do with your pay!'

The people were on the tiptoe of expectation, all wondering about John, whether perhaps he was the Messiah, but he spoke out and said to them all: 'I baptize you with water; but there is one to come who is mightier than I. I am not fit to unfasten his shoes. He will baptize you with the Holy Spirit and with fire.'

◆

In this next passage, St John baptizes Jesus.

St Matthew's Gospel, chapter 3, verses 13–17

Then Jesus arrived at the Jordan from Galilee, and came to John to be baptized by him. John tried to dissuade him. 'Do you come to me?' he said; 'I need rather to be baptized by you.' Jesus replied, 'Let it be so for the present; we do well to conform in this way with all that God requires.' John then allowed him to come. After baptism Jesus came up out of the water at once, and at that moment heaven opened; he saw the Spirit of God descending like a dove to alight upon him; and a voice from heaven was heard saying, 'This is my Son, my Beloved, on whom my favour rests.'

Day 3

Before embarking on his ministry, Jesus had to decide what kind of a leader he would be. He could have been a great politician or ruler. He could have been a great soldier, perhaps a terrorist rebel, who would overthrow the rule of the Roman Empire in Israel. He could have acquired great wealth by dazzling people with spectacular feats of daring and skill. He left the towns and went out into the wild countryside to think and pray. There he rejected all these possibilities as evil temptations.

St Luke's Gospel, chapter 4, verses 1–15 and 31–32

Full of the Holy Spirit, Jesus returned from the Jordan, and for forty days was led by the Spirit up and down the wilderness and tempted by the devil.

All that time he had nothing to eat, and at the end of it he was famished. The devil said to him, 'If you are the Son of God, tell this stone to become bread.' Jesus answered, 'Scripture says, "Man cannot live on bread alone." '

Next the devil led him up and showed him in a flash all the kingdoms of the world. 'All this dominion will I give to you,' he said, 'and the glory that goes with it; for it has been put in my hands and I can give it to anyone I choose. You have only to do homage to me and it shall all be yours.' Jesus answered him, 'Scripture says, "You shall do homage to the Lord your God and worship him alone." '

The devil took him to Jerusalem and set him on the parapet of the temple. 'If you are the Son of God,' he said, 'throw yourself down; for Scripture says, "He will give his angels orders to take care of you," and again, "They will support you in their arms for fear you should strike your foot against a stone." ' Jesus answered him, 'It has been said, "You are not to put the Lord your God to the test." '

So, having come to the end of all his temptations, the devil departed, biding his time.

Then Jesus, armed with the power of the Spirit, returned to Galilee; and reports about him spread through the whole countryside. He taught in their synagogues and all men sang his praises.

Coming down to Capernaum, a town in Galilee, he taught the people on the Sabbath, and they were astounded at his teaching, for what he said had the note of authority.

♦

In this anonymous passage, the writer discusses the life of Christ and what that achieved.

The life and achievement of Christ

Here is a man who was born in an obscure village, the child of a peasant woman. He grew up in another village. He worked in a carpenter's shop until he was thirty, and then for three years he was a travelling preacher.

He never wrote a book. He never held public office. He never went to college. He never owned a house. He never had a family. He never set foot inside a big city. He never travelled even two hundred miles from the place where he was born. He never did one of the things that usually accompany greatness. He had no credentials but himself. He had nothing to cope with this world except the naked power of his divine manhood.

While he was still a young man the tide of popular opinion turned against him. His friends ran away. One of them denied him. He was turned over to his enemies. He went through the mockery of a trial. He was nailed to a cross between two thieves. While he was dying his executioners gambled for the only piece of property he had while he was on this earth, and that was his coat. When he was dead, he was taken down and laid in a borrowed grave through the pity of a friend.

Nineteen hundred years have come and gone, and today he is the central figure of the human race.

I am well within the mark when I say that all the armies that ever marched, and all the navies that were ever built, and all the parliaments that ever met, and all the kings that ever reigned, put together, have not affected the life of man upon this earth as powerfully as has that *one solitary life.*

Day 4

Here are two stories which illustrate the magnetism of Jesus's character. In the first one he calls his disciples.

St Matthew's Gospel, chapter 4, verses 18–25

Jesus was walking by the Sea of Galilee when he saw two brothers, Simon called Peter and his brother Andrew, casting a net into the lake; for they were fishermen. Jesus said to them, 'Come with me, and I will make you fishers of men.' And at once they left their nets and followed him.

He went on, and saw another pair of brothers, James son of Zebedee and his brother John; they were in the boat with their father Zebedee, overhauling their nets.

He called them, and at once they left the boat and their father, and followed him.

He went round the whole of Galilee, teaching in the synagogues, preaching the gospel of the Kingdom, and curing whatever illness or infirmity there was among the people. His fame reached the whole of Syria; and sufferers from every kind of illness, racked with pain, possessed by devils, epileptic, or paralysed, were all brought to him, and he cured them. Great crowds also followed him, from Galilee and the Ten Towns, from Jerusalem and Judaea, and from Transjordan.

◆

St Luke's Gospel, chapter 19, verses 1–10

He entered Jericho and was passing through. And there was a man named Zacchaeus; he was a chief tax collector, and rich. And he sought to see who Jesus was, but he could not, on account of the crowd, because he was small of stature. So he ran on ahead and climbed up into a sycamore tree to see him, for he was to pass that way. And when Jesus came to the place, he looked up and said to him, 'Zacchaeus, make haste and come down; for I must stay at your house today.' So he made haste and came down, and received him joyfully.

And when they saw it they all murmured, 'He has gone in to be the guest of a man who is a sinner.'

And Zacchaeus stood and said to the Lord, 'Behold, Lord, the half of my goods I give to the poor; and if I have defrauded anyone of anything, I restore it fourfold.'

And Jesus said to him, 'Today salvation has come to this house, since he also is a son of Abraham. For the son of man came to seek and to save the lost.'

◆

Did Jesus smile to see the little man up the sycamore tree? His sense of humour and the joy of people like Zacchaeus is expressed in the following passage.

From Orthodoxy
by G K Chesterton

Joy, which was the small publicity of the pagan, is the gigantic secret of the Christian. The tremendous figure which fills the Gospels towers in this respect, as in every other, above all the thinkers who ever thought themselves tall. His pathos was natural, almost casual. The Stoics, ancient and modern, were proud of concealing their tears. He never concealed His tears; He showed them plainly on His open face at any daily sight, such as the far sight of His native city. Yet He concealed something. Solemn supermen and imperial diplomatists are proud of restraining their anger. He never restrained His anger. He flung furniture down the front steps of the Temple, and asked men how they expected to escape the damnation of Hell. Yet He restrained something. I say it with reverence; there was in that shattering personality a thread that must be called shyness. There was something that He hid from all men when He went up a mountain to pray. There was something that He covered constantly by abrupt silence or impetuous isolation. There was some one thing that was too great for God to show us when He walked upon our earth; and I have sometimes fancied that it was His mirth.

Day 5

This passage tells the story of Palm Sunday when Jesus came to Jerusalem, and how at first the crowds welcomed him.

St Matthew's Gospel, chapter 20, verses 17–19 and chapter 21, verses 1–11

Jesus was journeying towards Jerusalem, and on the way he took the Twelve aside, and said to them, 'We are now going to Jerusalem, and the son of Man will be given up to the chief priests and the doctors of the law; they will condemn him to death and hand him over to the foreign power, to be mocked and flogged and crucified, and on the third day he will be raised to life again.'

They were now nearing Jerusalem; and when they reached Bethphage at the Mount of Olives, Jesus sent two disciples with these instructions: 'Go to the village opposite, where you will at once find a donkey tethered with her foal beside her; untie them, and bring them to me. If anyone speaks to you, say, "Our Master needs them"; and he will let you take them at once.' This was to fulfil the prophecy which says, 'Tell the daughter of Zion, "Here is your king, who comes to you in gentleness, riding on an ass, riding on the foal of a beast of burden." '

The disciples went and did as Jesus had directed, and brought the donkey and her foal; they laid their cloaks on them and Jesus mounted. Crowds of people carpeted the road with their cloaks, and some cut branches from the trees to spread in his path. Then the crowd that went ahead and the others that came behind raised the shout: 'Hosanna to the Son of David! Blessings on him who comes in the name of the Lord! Hosanna in the heavens!'

When he entered Jerusalem the whole city went wild with excitement. 'Who is this?' people asked, and the crowd replied, 'This is the prophet Jesus, from Nazareth in Galilee.'

♦

In the following poem, the writer looks at the same events from a different point of view.

'The Donkey'
by G K Chesterton

When fishes flew and forests walk'd
And figs grew upon thorn,
Some moment when the moon was blood
Then surely I was born;
With monstrous head and sickening cry
And ears like errant wings,
The devil's walking parody
On all four-footed things.

The tatter'd outlaw of the earth,
Of ancient crooked will;
Starve, scourge, deride me: I am dumb,
I keep my secret still.

Fools! For I also had my hour;
One far fierce hour and sweet:
There was a shout about my ears,
And palms before my feet.

◆

Day 6

This passage describes the last supper that Christ had with his disciples before he was arrested.

St Matthew's Gospel, chapter 26, verses 14–29

Then one of the Twelve, the man called Judas Iscariot, went to the chief priests and said, 'What are you prepared to give me if I hand him over to you?' They paid him thirty silver pieces, and from then onwards he began to look for an opportunity to betray him.

Now on the first day of Unleavened Bread the disciples came to Jesus to say, 'Where do you want us to make the preparations for you to eat the Passover?' 'Go to a certain man in the city and say to him, "The Master says: My time is near. It is at your house that I am keeping Passover with my disciples." ' The disciples did what Jesus told them and prepared the Passover.

When evening came he was at table with the twelve disciples. And while they were eating he said, 'In truth I tell you, one of you is about to betray me.' They were greatly distressed and started asking him in turn, 'Not me, Lord, surely?' He answered, 'Someone who has dipped his hand into the dish with me, will betray me. The Son of Man is going to his fate, as the scriptures say he will, but alas for that man by whom the Son of Man is betrayed! Better for that man if he had never been born!' Judas, who was to betray him, asked in his turn, 'Not me, Rabbi, surely?' Jesus answered, 'It is you who say it.'

Now as they were eating, Jesus took some bread, and when he had said the blessing he broke it and gave it to the disciples. 'Take it and eat;' he said, 'this is my body.' Then he took a cup, and when he had given thanks he handed it to them saying, 'Drink all of you from this, for this is my blood, the blood of the covenant, poured out for many for the forgiveness of sins. From now on, I tell you, I shall never again drink wine until the day I drink the new wine with you in the kingdom of my Father.'

---◆---

Day 7

The following extracts describe how Jesus was betrayed by Judas and arrested by the Jewish authorities.

St Luke's Gospel, chapter 22, verses 39–54 and 63–65

Jesus came out, and went, as was his custom, to the Mount of Olives; and the disciples followed him. And when he came to the place he said to them, 'Pray that you may not enter into temptation.' And he withdrew from them about a stone's throw, and knelt down and prayed, 'Father, if you are willing, remove this cup from me; nevertheless not my will, but yours, be done.' And there appeared to him an angel from heaven, strengthening him. And being in an agony he prayed more earnestly; and his sweat became like great drops of blood falling down upon the ground. And when he rose from prayer, he came to the disciples and found them sleeping for sorrow, and

ιe said to them, 'Why do you sleep? Rise and pray that you may not
enter into temptation.'

While he was still speaking, there came a crowd, and the man
called Judas, one of the twelve, was leading them. He drew near to
Jesus to kiss him; but Jesus said to him, 'Judas, would you betray the
Son of Man with a kiss?' And when those who were about him saw
what would follow, they said, 'Lord, shall we strike with the sword?'
And one of them struck the slave of the high priest and cut off his
right ear. But Jesus said, 'No more of this!' And he touched his ear
and healed him. Then Jesus said to the chief priests and captains of
the temple and elders, who had come out against him, 'Have you
come out as against a robber, with swords and clubs? When I was
with you day after day in the temple, you did not lay hands on me.
But this is your hour, and the power of darkness.'

Then they seized him and led him away, bringing him into the
high priest's house.

Now the men who were holding Jesus mocked him and beat him;
they also blindfolded him and asked him, 'Prophesy! Who is it that
struck you?' And they spoke many other words against him, reviling
him.

♦

*Among the crowds who now denounced Jesus there were perhaps
some who had at first welcomed him to Jerusalem. This perversity in
public opinion is expressed in the following poem.*

'The Merchant's Carol'
by Frank Kendon

As we rode down the steep hillside,
Twelve merchants with our fairing,
A shout across the hollow land
Came loud upon our hearing,
A shout, a song, a thousand strong,
A thousand lusty voices:
'Make haste,' said I, I knew not why,
'Jerusalem rejoices!'

Beneath the olives fast we rode,
And louder came the shouting:
'So great a noise must mean,' said we,
'A king, beyond all doubting,'
Spurred on, did we, this king to see,
And left the mules to follow;
And nearer, clearer rang the noise
Along the Kidron hollow.

Behold a many-coloured crowd
About the gate we found there;
But one among them all, we marked,
One man who made no sound there;
Still louder ever rose the crowd's
'Hosanna in the highest!'
'O King,' thought I, 'I know not why
In all this joy thou sighest.'

Then he looked up, he looked at me
But whether he spoke I doubted:
How could I hear so calm a speech
When all the rabble shouted?
And yet these words, it seems, I heard:
'I shall be crowned tomorrow.'
They struck my heart with sudden smart,
And filled my bones with sorrow.

We followed far, we traded not,
But long we could not find him.
The very folk that called him king
Let robbers go and bind him.
We found him then, the sport of men,
Still calm among their crying;
And well we knew his words were true -
He was most kindly dying.

Day 8

The following passage tells the story of the crucifixion of Christ.

Extracts from St Matthew's Gospel, Chapter 27

Jesus, then, was brought before the governor, and the governor put to him this question, 'Are you the king of the Jews?' Jesus replied, 'It is you who say it.' But when he was accused by the chief priests and the elders he refused to answer at all. Pilate then said to him, 'Do you not hear how many charges they have brought against you?' But to the governor's complete amazement, he offered not a word to any of the charges.

At festival time it was the governor's practice to release a prisoner for the people, anyone they chose. Now there was at that time a notorious prisoner whose name was Barabbas. So when the crowd gathered, Pilate said to them, 'Which do you want me to release for you: Barabbas, or Jesus who is called Christ?' For Pilate knew it was out of jealousy that they had handed him over.

Now as he was seated in the chair of judgement, his wife sent him a message, 'Have nothing to do with that man; I have been upset all day by a dream I had about him.'

The chief priests and the elders, however, had persuaded the crowd to demand the release of Barabbas and the execution of Jesus. So when the governor spoke and asked them, 'Which of the two do you want me to release for you?', they said, 'Barabbas.' 'But in that case,' Pilate said to them, 'what am I to do with Jesus who is called Christ?' They all said, 'Let him be crucified!' 'Why?' he asked, 'What harm has he done?' But they shouted all the louder, 'Let him be crucified!' Then Pilate saw that he was making no impression, that in fact a riot was imminent. So he took some water, washed his hands in front of the crowd and said, 'I am innocent of this man's blood. It is your concern.' And the people, to a man, shouted back, 'His blood be on us and on our children!' Then he released Barabbas for them. He ordered Jesus to be first scourged and then handed over to be crucified.

Then the governor's soldiers took Jesus with them into the Praetorium and collected the whole cohort round him. And they stripped him and made him wear a scarlet cloak, and having twisted some thorns into a crown they put this on his head and placed a reed in his right hand. To make fun of him they knelt to him saying, 'Hail, king of the Jews!' And they spat on him and took the reed and struck him on the head with it. And when they had finished making fun of him, they took off the cloak and dressed him in his own clothes and led him away to crucify him.

On their way out, they came across a man from Cyrene, Simon by name, and enlisted him to carry his cross. When they had reached a place called Golgotha, that is, the place of the skull, they gave Jesus wine to drink mixed with gall, which he tasted but refused to drink. When they had finished crucifying him they shared out his clothing by casting lots, and then sat down and stayed there keeping guard over him.

Above his head was placed the charge against him; it read: 'This is Jesus, the King of the Jews.' Then two bandits were crucified with him, one on the right and one on the left.

From the sixth hour there was darkness over all the land until the ninth hour. And about the ninth hour, Jesus cried out in a loud voice, 'Eli, Eli, lama sabach-thani?' that is, 'My God, my God, why have you forsaken me?' When some of those who stood there heard this, they said, 'The man is calling on Elijah', and one of them quickly ran to get a sponge which he dipped in vinegar and, putting it on a reed, gave it him to drink. 'Wait!' said the rest of them, 'and see if Elijah will come to save him.' But Jesus, again crying out in a loud voice, yielded up his spirit.

And suddenly the veil of the sanctuary was torn in two from top to bottom; the earth quaked; the rocks were split; the tombs opened and the bodies of many holy men rose from the dead, and these, after his resurrection, came out of the tombs, entered the Holy City and appeared to a number of people. Meanwhile the centurion, together with the others guarding Jesus, had seen the earthquake and all that was taking place, and they were terrified and said, 'In truth this was a son of God.'

◆

The effect of Jesus on the people of his time and on many since is described by H G Wells.

From The Outline of History
by H G Wells

He was like some terrible moral huntsman digging mankind out of the snug burrows in which they had lived hitherto. In the white blaze of this kingdom of his there was to be no property, no privilege, no pride, no precedence; no motive indeed and no reward but love. Is it any wonder that men were dazzled and blinded and cried out against him? Even his disciples cried out when he would not spare them the light. Is it any wonder that the priests realized that between this man and themselves there was no choice but that he or witch-craft should perish? Is it any wonder that the Roman soldiers, confronted and amazed by something soaring over their comprehensions and threatening all their disciplines, should take refuge in wild laughter, and crown him with thorns, and robe him in purple to make a mock-Caesar of him? For to take him seriously was to enter a strange and alarming life, to abandon habits, to control instincts and impulses, to essay an incredible happiness.

———◆———

Day 9

In these extracts from a story called The Lion, the Witch and the Wardrobe *by C S Lewis, the lion (who is called Aslan) is put to death by a witch and her attendant hags. In many ways, the death of Aslan recalls the crucifixion of Jesus.*

'The Triumph of the Witch'
by C S Lewis

'Bind him, I say!' repeated the White Witch. The Hags made a dart at him and shrieked with triumph when they found that he made no resistance at all. Then others – evil dwarfs and apes – rushed in to help them, and between them they rolled the huge lion over on his back and tied all his four paws together, shouting and cheering as if they had done something brave, though, had the Lion chosen, one of those paws could have been the death of them all. But he made no noise, even when the enemies, straining and tugging, pulled the cords so tight that they cut into his flesh. Then they began to drag him towards the Stone Table ...

And they surged round Aslan, jeering at him, saying things like 'Puss, Puss! Poor Pussy,' and 'How many mice have you caught today, Cat?' and 'Would you like a saucer of milk, Pussums?'...

'Muzzle him!' said the Witch. And even now, as they worked about his face putting on the muzzle, one bite from his jaws would have cost two or three of them their hands. But he never moved. And this seemed to enrage all that rabble. Everyone was at him now ... he was surrounded by the whole crowd of creatures kicking him, hitting him, spitting on him, jeering at him ...

When once Aslan had been tied (and tied so that he was really a mass of cords) on the flat stone, a hush fell on the crowd. Four Hags, holding four torches, stood at the corners of the Table ... The Witch began to whet her knife. It looked, when the gleam of the torchlight fell on it, as if the knife were made of stone, not of steel, and it was of a strange and evil shape.

At last she drew near. She stood by Aslan's head. Her face was working and twitching with passion, but he looked up at the sky, still quiet, neither angry nor afraid, but a little sad. Then, just before she gave the blow, she stooped down and said in a quivering voice, 'And now, who has won? Fool, did you think that by all this you would save the human traitor?'

Day 10

The passage which follows tells the story of Christ's resurrection.

St Mark's Gospel, chapter 16, verses 1–8

When the Sabbath was over, Mary of Magdala, Mary the mother of James, and Salome bought aromatic oils intending to go and anoint him; and very early on the Sunday morning, just after sunrise, they came to the tomb. They were wondering among themselves who would roll away the stone for them from the entrance to the tomb, when they looked up and saw that the stone, huge as it was, had been rolled back already. They went into the tomb, where they saw a youth sitting on the right-hand side, wearing a white robe; and they were dumbfounded. But he said to them, 'Fear nothing; you are looking for Jesus of Nazareth, who was crucified. He has been raised again; he is not here; look, there is the place where they laid him. But go and give this message to his disciples and Peter: "He is going on before you into Galilee; there you will see him, as he told you."' Then they went out and ran away from the tomb, beside themselves with terror.

And they delivered all these instructions briefly to Peter and his companions. Afterwards Jesus himself sent out by them from east to west the sacred and imperishable message of eternal salvation.

♦

In The Lion, the Witch and the Wardrobe *by C S Lewis, the lion (who is called Aslan) is put to death on a stone table by a witch. Next morning, two girls, Susan and Lucy (who have been his friends) visit the table.*

'Deeper Magic from before the Dawn of Time'
by C S Lewis

The rising of the sun had made everything look so different – all the colours and shadows were changed – that for a moment they didn't see the important thing. Then they did. The Stone Table was broken into two pieces by a great crack that ran down it from end to end; and there was no Aslan.

'Oh, oh, oh!' cried the two girls, rushing back to the Table. 'Oh, it's too bad', sobbed Lucy; 'they might have left the body alone.'

'Who's done it?' cried Susan. 'What does it mean? Is it more magic?'

'Yes!' said a great voice behind their backs. 'It is more magic.'

They looked round. There, shining in the sunrise, larger than they had seen him before, shaking his mane (for it had apparently grown again) stood Aslan himself.

'Oh, Aslan!' cried the children, staring up at him, almost as much frightened as they were glad.

'Aren't you dead then, dear Aslan?' said Lucy.

'Not now,' said Aslan.

'You're not – not a – ?' asked Susan in a shaky voice. She couldn't bring herself to say the word ghost. Aslan stooped his golden head and licked her forehead. The warmth of his breath and a rich sort of smell that seemed to hang about his hair came all over her.

'Do I look it?' he said.

'Oh, you're real, you're real! Oh, Aslan!' cried Lucy, and both girls flung themselves upon him and covered him with kisses.

'But what does it all mean?' asked Susan when they were somewhat calmer.

'It means', said Aslan, 'that though the Witch knew the Deep Magic, there is a magic deeper still which she did not know. Her knowledge goes back only to the dawn of time. But if she could have looked a little further back, into the stillness and the darkness before time dawned, she would have read there is a different incantation. She would have known that when a willing victim who had committed no treachery was killed in a traitor's stead, the Table would crack and Death itself would start working backwards. And now -' 'Oh yes. Now?' said Lucy, jumping up and clapping her hands.

'Oh, children,' said the Lion, 'I feel my strength coming back to me. Oh, children, catch me if you can!'

♦

In this poem, Christina Rossetti links the rising of life in the Spring with the rising of Christ from the dead at Easter time. We are reconciled to death because we see it as a part of the natural cycle. Only at the harvest, at the end of time, will the whole meaning of life become clear.

'Easter Monday'
by Christina Rossetti

Out in the rain a world is growing green,
On half the trees quick buds are seen
Where glued-up buds have been.
Out in the rain God's Acre stretches green,
Its harvest quick tho' still unseen:
For there the Life hath been.

If Christ hath died His brethren well may die,
Sing in the gate of death, lay by
This life without a sigh:
For Christ hath died and good it is to die;
To sleep when so He lays us by,
Then wake without a sigh.

Yea, Christ hath died, yea, Christ is risen again:
Wherefore both life and death grow plain
To us who wax and wane;
For Christ Who rose shall die no more again:
Amen: till He makes all things plain
Let us wax on and wane.

Day 11

The character of Christ is discussed in the following passage.

From The Door Wherein I Went
by Lord Hailsham

What exactly was Jesus like to meet? If one had been a fellow-guest when he asked himself to dinner with Zacchaeus, or when he was eating with the Pharisee, what sort of a man would one in fact have seen and spoken to? What was his conversation like? Having asked this question, I looked at the Gospel again, and quite suddenly a new portrait seemed to stare at me out of the pages. I had never previously thought of a laughing, joking Jesus, strong and active, fond of good company and a glass of wine, telling funny stories, using, as every good teacher does, paradox and exaggeration as among the most effective aids to instruction, applying nicknames to his friends, and holding his companions spellbound with his talk. And yet, it is a very odd thing that one does not think of him in these terms.

As I reflected upon this, I came to the conclusion that the first thing we must learn about him is that we should have been absolutely entranced by his company. The man whom they crucified was intensely fond of life, and intensely vital and vivacious. He did not wish to die. He was the last person to be associated with suffering.

They called him a winebibber. They abused him for the company he kept. What was it, do you suppose, that kept Mary at his feet when Martha was scurrying about getting the dinner? Was it a portentous commentary on Holy Scripture? I feel sure that it was simply that she found his company actually enthralling. When one begins to think of it, can one see anything but fun in calling the two enthusiastic brothers 'Sons of Thunder', or impetuous, chivalrous, heroic, but often blundering Simon, the Rock? Is there no hint of humour in the foolish virgins, or the unjust steward, or the camel who finds it impossible to get through the eye of a needle, or the comparison of the speck of dust and the great beam in the eye, or the picture of wicked old Tiberius getting back the penny with his ugly old face on it, or the mustard plant likened to a tree, or the trade unionists who complain at the end of the day that someone else has got by with only an hour's work for the whole day's wage? Once one reflects about this, the picture of Jesus suddenly comes to life. The tragedy of the Cross was not that they crucified a melancholy figure, full of moral precepts, ascetic and gloomy. He was not John the Baptist, and the Baptist acknowledged this. What they crucified was a young man, vital, full of life and the joy of it, the Lord of life itself, and even more the Lord of laughter, someone so utterly attractive that people followed him for the sheer fun of it.

The twentieth century needs to recapture the vision of this glorious and happy man whose mere presence filled his companions with delight. No pale Galilean he, but a veritable Pied Piper of Hamelin who would have the children laughing all round him and squealing with pleasure and joy as he picked them up.

When I am asked about the utility of Christianity I must point to the consolations of living your life in the companionship of this person who commands your love and adoration precisely because having been through it all and sympathising with it all he cheers you up and will not have you sad. Your shame at your own misdoings, and shortcomings, your sense of awe and fear of the divine majesty, your broken heart in the presence of sickness and bereavement melts in the presence of this person into the sheer wonder and delight which the happiness of his presence excites!

3

Some of Christ's parables

In this section most of the parables are from the Bible. The stories stand on their own.

Day 1

The following three stories all describe a very human characteristic. If someone loses something and then finds it, they treasure it all the more. Jesus uses this idea to suggest how much God values people who, having turned away from him, return to him.

The first two stories are simpler because the things lost are not human. In the famous story of the prodigal son the situation is complicated by the fact that there was also a good son who never left his father. His jealousy is understandable but unattractive.

One of the fascinations of these stories is the picture they paint of a loving, caring God.

St Luke's Gospel, chapter 15, verses 1–32

Another time, the tax-gatherers and other bad characters were all crowding in to listen to him; and the Pharisees and the doctors of the law began grumbling among themselves: 'This fellow,' they said, 'welcomes sinners and eats with them.' He answered them with this parable: 'If one of you has a hundred sheep and loses one of them, does he not leave the ninety-nine in the open pasture and go after the missing one until he has found it? How delighted he is then! He lifts it on his shoulders, and home he goes to call his friends and neighbours together. "Rejoice with me!" he cries. "I have found my lost sheep." In the same way, I tell you, there will be greater joy in heaven over one sinner who repents than over ninety-nine righteous people who do not need to repent.

'Or again, if a woman has ten silver pieces and loses one of them, does she not light the lamp, sweep out the house, and look in every corner till she has found it? And when she has, she calls her friends and neighbours together and says, "Rejoice with me! I have found the piece that I lost." In the same way, I tell you, there is joy among the angels of God over one sinner who repents.'

Again he said: 'There was once a man who had two sons; and the younger said to his father, "Father, give me my share of the property." So he divided his estate between them. A few days later the younger son turned the whole of his share into cash and left home for a distant country, where he squandered it in reckless living. He had spent it all, when a severe famine fell upon that country and he began to feel the pinch. So he went and attached himself to one of the local landowners, who sent him on to his farm to mind the pigs. He would have been glad to fill his belly with the pods that the pigs were eating; and no one gave him anything. Then he came to his senses and said, "How many of my father's paid servants have more food than they can eat, and here am I, starving to death! I will set off and go to my father, and say to him, 'Father, I have sinned, against God and against you; I am no longer fit to be called your son; treat me as one of your paid servants.' " So he set out for his father's house. But while he was still a long way off his father saw him, and his heart went out to him. He ran to meet him, flung his arms round him, and kissed him. The son said, "Father, I have sinned, against God and against you; I am no longer fit to be called your son." But the father said to his servants, "Quick! fetch a robe, my best one, and put it on him; put a ring on his finger and shoes on his feet. Bring the fatted calf and kill it, and let us have a feast to celebrate the day. For this son of mine was dead and has come back to life; he was lost and is found." And the festivities began.

'Now the elder son was out on the farm; and on his way back, as he approached the house, he heard music and dancing. He called one of the servants and asked what it meant. The servant told him, "Your brother has come home, and your father has killed the fatted calf because he has him back safe and sound." But he was angry and refused to go in. His father came out and pleaded with him; but he retorted, 'You know how I have slaved for you all these years; I never once disobeyed your orders; and you never gave me so much as a kid, for a feast with my friends. But now that this son of yours turns up, after running through your money with his women, you kill the fatted calf for him." "My boy," said the father, "you are always with me, and everything I have is yours. How could we help celebrating this happy day? Your brother here was dead and has come back to life, was lost and is found." '

Day 2

The parable of the sower recalls a time when seeds were scattered in fields by hand. The story Jesus tells about this describes different reactions to his own teaching, but it is equally true of all teaching. Only willing learners can be taught.

St Mark's Gospel, chapter 4, verses 1–9 and 14–20

On another occasion he began to teach by the lake-side. The crowd that gathered round him was so large that he had to get into a boat on the lake, and there he sat, with the whole crowd on the beach right down to the water's edge. And he taught them many things by parables.

As he taught he said: 'Listen! A sower went out to sow. And it happened that as he sowed, some seed fell along the footpath; and the birds came and ate it up. Some seed fell on rocky ground, where it had little soil, and it sprouted quickly because it had no depth of earth; but when the sun rose the young corn was scorched, and as it had no root it withered away. Some seed fell among thistles; and the thistles shot up and choked the corn, and it yielded no crop. And some of the seed fell into good soil, where it came up and grew, and bore fruit; and the yield was thirtyfold, sixtyfold, even a hundredfold.' He added, 'If you have ears to hear, then hear.'

'The sower sows the word. Those along the footpath are people in whom the word is sown, but no sooner have they heard it than Satan comes and carries off the word which has been sown in them. It is the same with those who receive the seed on rocky ground; as soon as they hear the word, they accept it with joy, but it strikes no root in them; they have no staying-power; then, when there is trouble or persecution on account of the word, they fall away at once. Others again receive the seed among thistles; they hear the word, but worldly cares and the false glamour of wealth and all kinds of evil desire come in and choke the word, and it proves barren. And there are those who receive the seed in good soil; they hear the word and welcome it; and they bear fruit thirtyfold, sixtyfold, or a hundredfold.'

Day 3

This is one of the most well-loved of all Christ's parables. It describes true, disinterested loving kindness.

St Luke's Gospel, chapter 10, verses 25–37

On one occasion a lawyer came forward to put this test question to him: 'Master, what must I do to inherit eternal life?' Jesus said, 'What is written in the Law? What is your reading of it?' He replied, 'Love the Lord your God with all your heart, with all your soul, with all your strength, and with all your mind; and your neighbour as yourself.' 'That is the right answer,' said Jesus; 'do that and you will live.'

But he wanted to vindicate himself, so he said to Jesus, 'And who is my neighbour?' Jesus replied, 'A man was on his way from Jerusalem down to Jericho when he fell in with robbers, who stripped him, beat him, and went off leaving him half dead. It so happened that a priest was going down by the same road; but when he saw him, he went past on the other side. So too a Levite came to the place, and when he saw him went past on the other side. But a Samaritan who was making the journey came upon him, and when he saw him was moved to pity. He went up and bandaged his wounds, bathing them with oil and wine. Then he lifted him on to his own beast, brought him to an inn, and looked after him there. Next day he produced two silver pieces and gave them to the innkeeper, and said, "Look after him; and if you spend any more, I will repay you on my way back." Which of these three do you think was neighbour to the man who fell into the hands of the robbers?' He answered, 'The one who showed him kindness.' Jesus said, 'Go and do as he did.'

♦

The following extract comes from Daniel Miller's lecture about his work with young people. He responds to the feeling that the world's problems are too great for our puny efforts to make a difference.

From the Francis C Scott lecture given by Daniel Miller

There is so much to do; the problems seem to multiply faster than we can keep up with them; for every youth we touch there are thousands we will never see.

The answer is in each of us. We will choose, each of us, whether the issue is too big to confront. We will choose, each of us, whether we will take a stand for altering the condition of our children. We will choose, each of us, whether we will turn the other way and hide.

I am reminded of a man who was walking down a long stretch of beach. He observed a figure in the distance who seemed to be running back and forth down to the water doing a kind of dance. As he came closer he saw it was a young man, and he was not dancing. He was bending down picking up something from the sand, running to the water's edge, and throwing it into the sea.

When the man was close enough he stopped and asked the young man what he was doing.

'I'm picking up these starfish and saving them by throwing them back into the water,' he replied.

'But there are thousands of starfish on this beach. What possible difference can you be making?'

The young man did not say anything. He ran along the beach, bent down, picked up a starfish, ran down to the water, flung it into the sea, and returned to his questioner.

'It made a big difference for that one.'

Day 4

This parable describes the injustice of extremes of wealth and poverty, and the dangers of being so involved in our own possessions and self-indulgence that we forget the needs of other people.

St Luke's Gospel, chapter 16, verses 19–31

'There was once a rich man, who dressed in purple and the finest linen, and feasted in great magnificence every day. At his gate, covered with sores, lay a poor man named Lazarus, who would have been glad to satisfy his hunger with the scraps from the rich man's table. Even the dogs used to come and lick his sores. One day the poor man died and was carried away by the angels to be with Abraham. The rich man also died and was buried, and in Hades, where he was in torment, he looked up; and there, far away, was Abraham with Lazarus close beside him. "Abraham, my father," he called out, "take pity on me! Send Lazarus to dip the tip of his finger in water to cool my tongue, for I am in agony in this fire." But Abraham said, "Remember, my child, that all the good things fell to you while you were alive, and all the bad to Lazarus; now he has his consolation here and it is you who are in agony. But that is not all: there is a great chasm fixed between us; no one from our side who wants to reach you can cross it, and none may pass from your side to us." "Then, father," he replied, "will you send him to my father's house, where I have five brothers, to warn them, so that they too may not come to this place of torment?" But Abraham said, "They have Moses and the prophets; let them listen to them." "No, father Abraham," he replied, "but if someone from the dead visits them, they will repent." Abraham answered, "If they do not listen to Moses and the prophets they will pay no heed even if someone should rise from the dead." '

Day 5

In this parable God's mercy is contrasted with the selfish jealousy of the labourers.

St Matthew's Gospel, chapter 20, verses 1–16

'The kingdom of Heaven is like this. There was once a landowner who went out early one morning to hire labourers for his vineyard; and after agreeing to pay them the usual day's wage he sent them off to work. Going out three hours later he saw some more men standing idle in the market-place. "Go and join the others in the vineyard," he said, "and I will pay you a fair wage"; so off they went. At midday he went out again, and at three in the afternoon, and made the same arrangement as before. An hour before sunset he went out and found another group standing there; so he said to them, "Why are you standing about like this all day with nothing to do?" "Because no one has hired us," they replied; so he told them, "Go and join the others in the vineyard." When evening fell, the owner of the vineyard said to his steward, "Call the labourers and give them their pay, beginning with those who came last and ending with the first." Those who had started work an hour before sunset came forward, and were paid the full day's wage. When it was the turn of the men who had come first, they expected something extra, but were paid the same amount as the others. As they took it, they grumbled at their employer: "These latecomers have done only one hour's work, yet you have put them on a level with us, who have sweated the whole day long in the blazing sun!" The owner turned to one of them and said, "My friend, I am not being unfair to you. You agreed on the usual wage for the day, did you not? Take your pay and go home. I choose to pay the last man the same as you. Surely I am free to do what I like with my own money. Why be jealous because I am kind?" Thus will the last be first, and the first last.'

Day 6

A 'talent' was originally a coin. In earlier translations of this parable the man, who represents God, gave each man some talents. Hence the modern meaning of the word. In this recent translation the coins are described as bags of gold. This story shows the importance of everybody developing their own talents to fulfil their purpose in life.

St Matthew's Gospel, chapter 25, verses 14–30

The kingdom of heaven is like a man going abroad, who called his servants and put his capital in their hands; to one he gave five bags of gold, to another two, to another one, each according to his capacity. Then he left the country. The man who had five bags went at once and employed them in business, and made a profit of five bags, and the man who had the two bags made two. But the man who had been given one bag of gold went off and dug a hole in the ground, and hid his master's money. A long time afterwards their master returned, and proceeded to settle accounts with them. The man who had been given the five bags of gold came and produced the five he had made: 'Master,' he said, 'you left five bags with me; look, I have made five more.' 'Well done, my good and trusty servant!' said the master. 'You have proved trustworthy in a small way; I will now put you in charge of something big. Come and share your master's delight.' The man with the two bags then came and said, 'Master, you left two bags with me; look, I have made two more.' 'Well done, my good and trusty servant!' said the master. 'You have proved trustworthy in a small way; I will now put you in charge of something big. Come and share your master's delight.' Then the man who had been given one bag came and said, 'Master, I knew you to be a hard man: you reap where you have not sown, you gather where you have not scattered; so I was afraid, and I went and hid your gold in the ground. Here it is – you have what belongs to you.' 'You lazy rascal!' said the master. 'You knew that I reap where I have not sown, and gather where I have not scattered? Then you ought to have put my money on deposit, and on my return I should have got it back with interest. Take the bag of gold from him, and give it to the one with the ten bags. For the man who has will always be given more, till he has enough to spare; and the man who has not will forfeit even what he has. Fling the useless servant out into the dark, the place of wailing and grinding of teeth!'

♦

The following story is related to the parable of the talents.

The tumbler
by R H Lloyd

Long ago there lived a tumbler who travelled from fair to fair across the countryside, earning his livelihood entertaining the crowds. He was very skilled and always drew large numbers of spectators who loved to watch him juggling with plates and clubs and balls and performing all sorts of breath-taking acrobatics.

At the height of his powers, he fell sick and managed to make his way to a monastery where he was nursed back to health.

The tumbler was so impressed with the love and care lavished on him by the monks that he decided he too would like to become a monk. He was placed under the guidance of a senior monk, called the Novice Master, who was responsible for the training of beginners.

'Now,' said the Novice Master, 'we shall start you off in the Library. I know that the librarian has been short-handed and would like some help.'

But the tumbler didn't know the first thing about manuscripts and couldn't read Latin, the language in which the manuscripts were written. He turned out to be more of a hindrance than a help, although he tried very hard. Eventually the librarian went to see the Novice Master.

'You must take him away,' he pleaded. 'He is totally unsuited for any work in the Library.'

The Novice Master took the tumbler to the Scriptorium where he was given some writing material and a quill pen, and some simple copying work to do. But he had difficulty holding the pen and made mistake after mistake. After less than a week he had to be moved.

The tumbler was taken to the Chapel and left with the choir-master, in the hope that he might be trained as a singer. The choir-master persevered for many weeks, but in the end he gave up.

'You must take him away,' he begged. 'He's ruining every service. I've never met anyone so unmusical.'

Next he was transferred to the kitchens. But here again, try as he might, he made mistake after mistake. He forgot to add salt when boiling vegetables. He burnt the meat. He used the wrong pots and pans. After a month the chef called on the Novice Master.

'You must take that tumbler away from the kitchen,' he said in desperation. 'He means well and he tries hard, but he is completely chaotic. Nothing is in its proper place, and I just don't know what calamity to expect next.'

He was transferred from the kitchens to the farm, from the farm to the dispensary, from the dispensary to the wine-cellars; but the story was always the same.

'Please take the tumbler away from here. He's a nice man, he tries hard, we all like him, but – please move him somewhere else.'

The twelve months passed by and the tumbler knew that his interview with the Abbot regarding his suitability was drawing near.

'I'm a failure,' he thought to himself sadly. 'I have no gift to offer God like the other monks. I can't sing, I can't write, I can't read Latin; I can't cook; I can't mix herbs for medicine; I'm useless. O God,' he prayed, 'I wish I had a gift I could offer you.'

At that moment a marvellous idea swept through his mind. 'I know what I'll do,' he said to himself, and hurried off to the Chapel.

He walked up the length of the Chapel and stood in front of the altar and bowed low. Then, removing his habit, he began to tumble. He went through his whole range of acrobatics with tremendous skill, and juggled balls, plates and clubs faster than the eye could see.

During the performance, one of the monks happened to enter the Chapel, and saw the tumbler in action. He rushed off to the Abbot's study. Bursting in, he gasped, 'Father Abbot, come quickly. The tumbler has gone out of his mind. He's gone mad! He's performing acrobatics in the Chapel, in front of the altar of all places!'

The Abbot accompanied the monk to the Chapel. There, sure enough, the tumbler was giving the exhibition of his life, with an expression of pure joy on his face. The Abbot stood and watched. The monk plucked his sleeve and whispered urgently, 'Aren't you going to put a stop to this dreadful behaviour in the Chapel?'

'Shsh!' replied the Abbot, putting his finger to his lips, and continued to watch with evident pleasure.

After a while the Abbot turned, and beckoning to the monk, quietly left the Chapel.

'Father Abbot!' protested the monk. 'Why didn't you stop that man and reprimand him for behaving so irreverently in God's presence?'

'Ah,' said the Abbot with a gentle smile, 'you don't understand, do you? Can't you see that the tumbler is offering the only thing he is good at to God? And, what's more I'm sure that God is delighted with his offering!'

A few days later when the tumbler appeared before the Abbot, he was surprised by the warmth of his welcome. He really expected to be told that he wasn't suited to the life of the monastery. Instead he heard the Abbot say to him, 'If you still wish to stay with us, you are very welcome. I am sure that we shall all enjoy being entertained by you from time to time. It will be quite a change having a tumbler as one of our members.'

Day 7

In this parable, Jesus suggests that many people do not leave enough time in their lives for developing the spiritual side of their characters; they do not leave enough time for God.

St Luke's Gospel, chapter 14, verses 15–24

One of the company, after hearing all this, said to him, 'Happy the man who shall sit at the feast in the kingdom of God!' Jesus answered, 'A man was giving a big dinner party and had sent out many invitations. At dinner time he sent his servant with a message for his guests, "Please come, everything is now ready." They began one and all to excuse themselves. The first said, "I have bought a piece of land, and I must go and look over it; please accept my apologies." The second said, "I have bought five yoke of oxen, and I am on my way to try them out; please accept my apologies." The next said, "I have just got married and for that reason I cannot come." When the servant came back he reported this to his master. The master of the house was angry and said to him, "Go out quickly into the streets and alleys of the town, and bring me in the poor, the crippled, the blind, and the lame." The servant said, "Sir, your orders have been carried out and there is still room." The master replied, "Go out onto the highways and along the hedgerows and make them come in; I want my house to be full. I tell you that not one of those who were invited shall taste my banquet."'

◆

The following poem is also about making time for God..

From Prayers of Life
by Michel Quoist

I went out, Lord.
Men were coming out,
They were coming and going,
Walking and running.

Everything was rushing, cars, lorries, the street, the whole town.
Men were rushing not to waste time.
They were rushing after time,
To catch up with time,
To gain time.

Goodbye, sir, excuse me, I haven't time.
I'll come back, I can't wait, I haven't time.
I must end this letter – I haven't time.
I'd love to help you, but I haven't time.
I can't accept, having no time.
I can't think, I can't read, I am swamped, I haven't time.
I'd like to pray, but I haven't time.
You understand, Lord, they simply haven't the time.

The child is playing, he hasn't time right now... Later on...
The schoolboy has his homework to do, he hasn't time... Later on...
The student has his courses, and so much work, he hasn't time...
Later on...
The young man is at his sports, he hasn't time... Later on...
The young married man has his new house, he has to fix it up,
he hasn't time... Later on...
The grandparents have their grandchildren, they haven't time...
Later on...
They are ill, they have their treatments, they haven't time...
Later on...
They are dying, they have no...
Too late!... They have no more time!
And so all men run after time, Lord...

You who are beyond time, Lord... you know what you are doing.
You make no mistakes in your distribution of time to men.
You give each one time to do what you want him to do.
But we must not lose time
waste time
kill time,
For time is a gift that you give us,
But a perishable gift,
A gift that does not keep.

4

Some of Christ's miracles

◆

The readings in this section may best be used interspersed among those about the life of Christ (see section 2). They represent miracles of different kinds, and ones which point to some special aspect of faith. All but one reading are from the Bible. The remaining extract is a modern miracle which could be read alongside the story of blind Bartimaeus.

Day 1

This miracle is often referred to during Christian wedding services because it shows Jesus attending such a social event and wanting it to go well.

St John's Gospel, chapter 2, verses 1–11

On the third day there was a wedding at Cana-in-Galilee. The mother of Jesus was there, and Jesus and his disciples were guests also. The wine gave out, so Jesus's mother said to him, 'They have no wine left.' He answered, 'Your concern, mother, is not mine. My hour has not yet come.' His mother said to the servants, 'Do whatever he tells you.' There were six stone water-jars standing near, of the kind used for Jewish rites of purification; each held from twenty to thirty gallons. Jesus said to the servants, 'Fill the jars with water,' and they filled them to the brim. 'Now draw some off', he ordered, 'and take it to the steward of the feast'; and they did so. The steward tasted the water now turned into wine, not knowing its source; though the servants who had drawn the water knew. He hailed the bridegroom and said, 'Everyone serves the best wine first, and waits until the guests have drunk freely before serving the poorer sort; but you have kept the best wine till now.'

Day 2

When Jesus was alive, the country of Israel was a part of the Roman Empire. Many of the Jewish people hated this and hated the Roman soldiers who occupied their country. Some of these soldiers, however, befriended the Jews and adopted their religion. Such a one was the centurion in the following story. Although he was in a position of authority he was humble towards Jesus who, he thought, might not want to enter the house of a foreigner. Another endearing quality is his care for his servant.

St Luke's Gospel, chapter 7, verses 1–10

When he had finished addressing the people, he went to Capernaum. A centurion there had a servant whom he valued highly; this servant was ill and near to death. Hearing about Jesus, he sent some Jewish elders with the request that he would come and save his servant's life. They approached Jesus and pressed their petition earnestly: 'He deserves this favour from you,' they said, 'for he is a friend of our nation and it is he who built us our synagogue.' Jesus went with them; but when he was not far from the house, the centurion sent friends with this message: 'Do not trouble further, sir; it is not for me to have you under my roof, and that is why I did not presume to approach you in person. But say the word and my servant will be cured. I know, for in my position I am myself under orders, with soldiers under me. I say to one, "Go", and he goes; to another, "Come here", and he comes; and to my servant, "Do this", and he does it.' When Jesus heard this, he admired the man, and, turning to the crowd that was following him, he said, 'I tell you, nowhere, even in Israel, have I found faith like this.' And the messengers returned to the house and found the servant in good health.

Day 3

*The remarkable qualities revealed by Christ in the following story are
fearlessness and power.*

St Mark's Gospel, chapter 4, verses 35–41

That day, in the evening, he said to them, 'Let us cross over to the
other side of the lake.' So they left the crowd and took him with
them in the boat where he had been sitting; and there were other
boats accompanying him. A heavy squall came on and the waves
broke over the boat until it was all but swamped. Now he was in the
stern asleep on a cushion; they roused him and said, 'Master, we are
sinking! Do you not care?' He awoke, rebuked the wind, and said to
the sea, 'Hush! Be still!' The wind dropped and there was a dead
calm. He said to them, 'Why are you such cowards? Have you no
faith even now? They were awestruck and said to one another, 'Who
can this be? Even the wind and the sea obey him.'

Day 4

*To tell someone that their sins are forgiven is easy, but how do you
show that this has actually happened? The man in the following story
seems to have an illness which is associated with feelings of guilt or
shame. He does have good friends, however, who are determined to
get help for him. They are convinced that Jesus could provide that help
and they will go to any lengths to bring him into his presence. Jesus
can prove his ability to forgive sins by showing what effect this has on
the sick man.*

St Luke's Gospel, chapter 5, verses 17–26

One day he was teaching, and Pharisees and teachers of the law
were sitting round. People had come from every village of Galilee
and from Judaea and Jerusalem, and the power of the Lord was with
him to heal the sick. Some men appeared carrying a paralysed man
on a bed. They tried to bring him in and set him down in front of
Jesus, but finding no way to do so because of the crowd, they went

up onto the roof and let him down through the tiling, bed and all, into the middle of the company in front of Jesus. When Jesus saw their faith, he said, 'Man, your sins are forgiven you.'

The lawyers and the Pharisees began saying to themselves, 'Who is this fellow with his blasphemous talk? Who but God alone can forgive sins?' But Jesus knew what they were thinking and answered them: 'Why do you harbour thoughts like these? Is it easier to say, "Your sins are forgiven you", or to say, "Stand up and walk"? But to convince you that the Son of Man has the right on earth to forgive sins' – he turned to the paralysed man – 'I say to you, stand up, take your bed, and go home.' And at once he rose to his feet before their eyes, took up the bed he had been lying on, and went home praising God. They were all lost in amazement and praised God; filled with awe they said, 'You would never believe the things we have seen today.'

Day 5

No doubt Jairus, the man in the following story, was proud: he was president of the synagogue. But when it came to the life of his daughter all his pride was gone.

On his way to help, Jesus was hampered by the crowd and by a woman who should not have been outside at all, let alone touching people. The illness she had was considered to be unclean. But she had such faith she thought that just touching Jesus's cloak would cure her and she was sure that nobody would notice in the crowd.

St Luke's Gospel, chapter 8, verses 40–56

When Jesus returned, the people welcomed him, for they were all expecting him. Then a man appeared – Jairus was his name and he was president of the synagogue. Throwing himself down at Jesus's feet he begged him to come to his house, because he had an only daughter, about twelve years old, who was dying. And while Jesus was on his way he could hardly breathe for the crowds.

Among them was a woman who had suffered from haemorrhages for twelve years; and nobody had been able to cure her. She came up from behind and touched the edge of his cloak, and at once her haemorrhage stopped. Jesus said, 'Who was it that touched me?' All disclaimed it, and Peter and his companions said, 'Master, the crowds are hemming you in and pressing upon you!' But Jesus said, 'Someone did touch me, for I felt that power had gone out from me.' Then the woman, seeing that she was detected, came trembling and fell at his feet. Before all the people she explained why she had touched him and how she had been instantly cured. He said to her, 'My daughter, your faith has cured you. Go in peace.'

While he was still speaking, a man came from the president's house with the message, 'Your daughter is dead; trouble the Rabbi no further.' But Jesus heard, and interposed. 'Do not be afraid,' he said; 'only show faith and she will be well again.' On arrival at the house he allowed no one to go in with him except Peter, John, and James, and the child's father and mother. And all were weeping and lamenting for her. He said, 'Weep no more; she is not dead: she is asleep'; and they only laughed at him, well knowing that she was dead. But Jesus took hold of her hand and called her: 'Get up, my child.' Her spirit returned, she stood up immediately, and he told them to give her something to eat. Her parents were astounded but he forbade them to tell anyone what had happened.

Day 6

The next reading is a wonderful story of persistence and faith. Perhaps we should all take this course when pursuing what is good for us.

St Mark's Gospel, chapter 10, verses 46–52

They came to Jericho; and as he was leaving the town, with his disciples and a large crowd, Bartimaeus son of Timaeus, a blind beggar, was seated at the roadside. Hearing that it was Jesus of Nazareth, he began to shout, 'Son of David, Jesus, have pity on me!' Many of the people told him to hold his tongue; but he shouted all the more, 'Son of David, have pity on me.' Jesus stopped and said, 'Call him'; so they called the blind man and said, 'Take heart; stand up; he is calling you.' At that he threw off his cloak, sprang up, and came to Jesus. Jesus said to him, 'What do you want me to do for you?'

'Master,' the blind man answered, 'I want my sight back.' Jesus said to him, 'Go; your faith has cured you.' And at once he recovered his sight and followed him on the road.

♦

Bartimaeus had the light of faith but not of sight. Jesus gave him that. He used his new capacity to see, to follow Jesus.

This next story also describes a miracle of light, but it occurred nearly two thousand years later, in our own time, during a visit by the journalist Malcolm Muggeridge to film Mother Teresa in Calcutta.

From Something Beautiful for God
by Malcolm Muggeridge

There was another actual miracle. Part of the work of the Sisters is to pick up the dying from the streets of Calcutta, and bring them into a building given to Mother Teresa for the purpose (a sometime temple dedicated to the cult of the goddess Kali), there, as she puts it, to die within sight of a loving face. Some do die; others survive and are cared for. This Home for the Dying is dimly lit by small windows high up in the walls, and Ken was adamant that filming was quite impossible there. We had only one small light with us, and to get the place adequately lighted in the time at our disposal was quite impossible. It was decided that, nonetheless, Ken should have a go, but by way of insurance he took, as well, some film in an outside courtyard where some of the inmates were sitting in the sun. In the processed film, the part taken inside was bathed in a particularly beautiful soft light, whereas the part taken outside was rather dim and confused.

How to account for this? Ken has all along insisted that, technically speaking, the result is impossible. To prove the point, on his next filming expedition – to the Middle East – he used some of the same stock in a similarly poor light, with completely negative results. He offers no explanation, but just shrugs and agrees that it happened. I myself am absolutely convinced that the technically unaccountable light is, in fact, the Kindly Light Newman refers to in his well-known exquisite hymn – now, as I have read, barred from up-to-day hymnals as being unduly pessimistic. Mother Teresa's Home for the Dying is overflowing with love, as one senses immediately on entering it. This love is luminous, like the haloes artists have seen and made visible round the heads of the saints. I find it not at all surprising that the luminosity should register on a photographic film. The supernatural is only an infinite projection of the natural, as the furthest horizon is an image of eternity. Jesus put mud on a blind man's eyes and made him see. It was a beautiful gesture, showing that he could bring out even in mud its innate power to heal and enrich. All the wonder and glory of mud – year by year giving creatures their food, and our eyes the delight of flowers and trees and blossoms – was crystallized to restore sight to unseeing eyes.

One thing everyone who has seen the film seems to be agreed about is that the light in the Home for the Dying is quite exceptionally lovely. This is, from every point of view, highly appropriate. Dying derelicts from the streets might normally be supposed to be somewhat repellent, giving off stenches, emitting strange groans. Actually, if the Home for the Dying were piled high with flowers and resounding with musical chants – as it may well have been in its Kali days – it could not be more restful and serene. So, the light conveys perfectly what the place is really like; an outward and visible luminosity manifesting God's inward and invisible omnipresent love. This is precisely what miracles are for – to reveal the inner reality of God's outward creation. I am personally persuaded that Ken recorded the first authentic photographic miracle.

It so delighted me that I fear I talked and wrote about it to the point of tedium, and sometimes of irritation. Miracles are unpopular today – to the scientifically minded because they seem to conflict with so-called scientific miracles, like bumping television programmes across the world by satellite, or going to the moon; to the ostensibly religiously minded because they remind them of miraculous claims made in the past and now discredited, which they wish to forget. Once, out at Hatch End, where Father Agnellus Andrew has his estimable set-up for instructing Roman Catholic priests and prelates in the techniques of radio and television, Peter Chafer and I showed our Mother Teresa film to a gathering of ecclesiastical brass. Afterwards, I spoke about the miracle of the light in the Home for the Dying. It troubled them, I could see. They did not want to hear about it. One or two hazarded an opinion that, no doubt, the result was due to some accidental adjustment in the camera or quality in the stock. They were happy when we moved on to other topics. In Graham Greene's brilliant satirical play *The Potting-Shed*, he explores the theme of a free-thinking family in which a miracle occurs, and of the lengths they go to in covering up all trace of the miraculous occurrence. He can scarcely have expected to live to see the converse situation – Roman Catholics as assiduously covering up, or at any rate ignoring, a miraculous occurrence in Mother Teresa's Home for the Dying. I record the matter here in the hope that, in years to come, Christian believers may be glad to know that in a dark time the light that shone about the heads of dying derelicts brought in from the streets of Calcutta by Mother Teresa's Sisters of the Missionaries of Charity, somehow got itself recorded on film.

5

The story of Saint Peter

If we pick out the stories about St Peter from the New Testament we see that this man, who did so much to found the Christian Church and change the course of history, had many failings. It is thought that he is the source of much of St Mark's information about Jesus's life and sayings in the Gospel. If so, he never hesitated to tell stories against himself as though to show that even those who feel inadequate should not give up in their search for God and that Christ can transform people into fit instruments for carrying out his work.

Day 1

In this first story St Peter, originally called Simon and only later given the name Peter by Jesus, considers himself thoroughly unworthy in the presence of Christ. But when he is called, he impulsively follows.

St Luke's Gospel, chapter 5, verses 1–11

One day as he stood by the Lake of Gennesaret, and the people crowded upon him to listen to the word of God, he noticed two boats lying at the water's edge; the fishermen had come ashore and were washing their nets. He got into one of the boats, which belonged to Simon, and asked him to put out a little way from the shore; then he went on teaching the crowds from his seat in the boat. When he had finished speaking, he said to Simon, 'Put out into deep water and let down your nets for a catch.' Simon answered, 'Master, we were hard at work all night and caught nothing at all; but if you say so, I will let down the nets.' They did so and made a big haul of fish; and their nets began to split. So they signalled to their partners in the other boat to come and help them. This they did, and loaded both boats to the point of sinking. When Simon saw what had happened he fell at Jesus's knees and said, 'Go, Lord, leave me, sinner that I am!' For he and all his companions were amazed at the catch they had made; so too were his partners James and John, Zebedee's sons. 'Do not be afraid,' said Jesus to Simon; 'from now on you will be catching men.' As soon as they had brought the boats to land, they left everything and followed him.

Day 2

The following story shows both the strength and the limitations of St Peter's faith.

St Matthew's Gospel, chapter 14, verses 22–33

Then he made the disciples embark and go on ahead to the other side, while he sent the people away; after doing that, he went up the hill-side to pray alone. It grew late, and he was there by himself. The boat was already some furlongs from the shore, battling with a head-wind and a rough sea. Between three and six in the morning he came to them, walking over the lake. When the disciples saw him walking on the lake they were so shaken that they cried out in terror: 'It is a ghost!' But at once he spoke to them: 'Take heart! It is I, do not be afraid.'

Peter called to him: 'Lord, if it is you, tell me to come to you over the water.' 'Come,' said Jesus. Peter stepped down from the boat, and walked over the water towards Jesus. But when he saw the strength of the gale he was seized with fear; and beginning to sink, he cried, 'Save me, Lord.' Jesus at once reached out and caught hold of him, and said, 'Why did you hesitate? How little faith you have!' They then climbed into the boat, and the wind dropped. And the men in the boat fell at his feet, exclaiming, 'Truly you are the Son of God.'

♦

Despite Peter's limitations, Jesus recognizes his strong, loving charac-ter. These are the qualities which God will use and to which Jesus gives the name Peter, which means a rock.

St Matthew's Gospel, chapter 16, verses 13–20

When he came to the territory of Caesarea Philippi, Jesus asked his disciples, 'Who do men say that the Son of Man is?' They answered,

'Some say John the Baptist, others Elijah, others Jeremiah, or one of the prophets.' 'And you,' he asked, 'who do you say I am?' Simon Peter answered: 'You are the Messiah, the Son of the living God.' Then Jesus said: 'Simon son of Jonah, you are favoured indeed! You did not learn that from mortal man; it was revealed to you by my heavenly Father. And I say this to you: You are Peter, the Rock; and on this rock I will build my church, and the powers of death shall never conquer it. I will give you the keys of the kingdom of Heaven; what you forbid on earth shall be forbidden in heaven, and what you allow on earth shall be allowed in heaven.' He then gave his disciples strict orders not to tell anyone that he was the Messiah.

Day 3

In this reading, St Peter expresses the desire most people have to avoid suffering and to have a happy ending. More than any of the other disciples, he seems to learn through his mistakes and it is interesting that he never seems to have made any effort to suppress these stories. This may have been because of his natural humility and desire that the whole truth should be told or because he also felt that others too could learn from his errors.

St Matthew's Gospel, chapter 16, verses 21–23

From that time Jesus began to make it clear to his disciples that he had to go to Jerusalem, and there to suffer much from the elders, chief priests, and doctors of the law; to be put to death and to be raised again on the third day. At this Peter took him by the arm and began to rebuke him: 'Heaven forbid!' he said. 'No, Lord, this shall never happen to you.' Then Jesus turned and said to Peter, 'Away with you, Satan; you are a stumbling-block to me. You think as men think, not as God thinks.'

♦

The next reading, the story of the transfiguration, shows how St Peter was so often the one to speak out, even in an alarming situation when he scarcely knew what to say.

St Luke's Gospel, chapter 9, verses 28–36

About eight days after this conversation he took Peter, John, and James with him and went up into the hills to pray. And while he was praying the appearance of his face changed and his clothes became dazzling white. Suddenly there were two men talking with him; these were Moses and Elijah, who appeared in glory and spoke of his departure, the destiny he was to fulfil in Jerusalem. Meanwhile Peter and his companions had been in a deep sleep; but when they awoke, they saw his glory and the two men who stood beside him. And as these were moving away from Jesus, Peter said to him, 'Master, how good it is that we are here! Shall we make three shelters, one for you, one for Moses, and one for Elijah?'; but he spoke without knowing what he was saying. The words were still on his lips, when there came a cloud which cast a shadow over them; they were afraid as they entered the cloud, and from it came a voice: 'This is my Son, my Chosen; listen to him.' When the voice had spoken, Jesus was seen to be alone. The disciples kept silence and at that time told nobody anything of what they had seen.

---◆---

Day 4

In this reading, Jesus shows that a position of power is one not of priv-ileges to be enjoyed but of hard work and service. Peter's reaction is, as usual, both affectionate and impulsive.

St John's Gospel, chapter 13, verses 1–17

It was before the Passover festival. Jesus knew that his hour had come and he must leave this world and go to the Father. He had always loved his own who were in the world, and now he was to show the full extent of his love.

The devil had already put it into the mind of Judas son of Simon Iscariot to betray him. During supper, Jesus, well aware that the Father had entrusted everything to him, and that he had come from God and was going back to God, rose from table, laid aside his garments, and taking a towel, tied it round him. Then he poured water into a basin, and began to wash his disciples' feet and to wipe them with the towel.

When it was Simon Peter's turn, Peter said to him, 'You, Lord, washing my feet?' Jesus replied, 'You do not understand now what I am doing, but one day you will.' Peter said, 'I will never let you wash my feet.' 'If I do not wash you,' Jesus replied, 'you are not in fellowship with me.' 'Then, Lord,' said Simon Peter, 'not my feet only; wash my hands and head as well!'

Jesus said, 'A man who has bathed needs no further washing; he is altogether clean; and you are clean, though not every one of you.' He added the words 'not every one of you' because he knew who was going to betray him.

After washing their feet and taking his garments again, he sat down. 'Do you understand what I have done for you?' he asked. 'You call me "Master" and "Lord", and rightly so, for that is what I am. Then if I, your Lord and Master, have washed your feet, you also ought to wash one another's feet. I have set you an example: you are to do as I have done for you. In very truth I tell you, a servant is not greater than his master, nor a messenger than the one who sent him. If you know this, happy are you if you act upon it.'

♦

This is the most poignant story about St Peter, when, after Jesus's arrest, Peter is too afraid to admit that he is one of the disciples. Consider the difference between this behaviour of a man who is basically good, and the behaviour of Judas, who has deliberately chosen the way of evil.

St Luke's Gospel, chapter 22, verses 54–62

Then they seized him and led him away, bringing him into the high priest's house. Peter followed at a distance; and when they had kindled a fire in the middle of the courtyard and sat down together, Peter sat among them. Then a maid, seeing him as he sat in the light and gazing at him, said, 'This man also was with him.' But he denied it, saying, 'Woman, I do not know him.' And a little later someone else saw him and said, 'You also are one of them.' But Peter said, 'Man, I am not.' And after an interval of about an hour still another insisted, saying, 'Certainly this man also was with him; for he is a Galilean.' But Peter said, 'Man, I do not know what you are saying.' And immediately, while he was still speaking, the cock crowed. And the Lord turned and looked at Peter. And Peter remembered the word of the Lord, how he had said to him, 'Before the cock crows today, you will deny me three times.' And he went out and wept bitterly.

Day 5

St Peter was one of the first disciples to see the empty tomb and to understand the resurrection of Christ. After this resurrection, Christ appeared to the disciples on several occasions. In this story, Jesus gives Peter his instructions to care for his followers who would form the nucleus of the Christian Church. The story recalls the first time when Jesus called Peter from his fishing to be a disciple. It also points forward to the story that Peter died while visiting the Christian Church in Rome. The authorities were going to crucify him but he said he was not worthy to die as Jesus did so he insisted on being crucified upside down.

St John's Gospel, chapter 21, verses 1–19

Some time later, Jesus showed himself to his disciples once again, by the Sea of Tiberias; and in this way. Simon Peter and Thomas 'the Twin' were together with Nathanael of Cana-in-Galilee. The sons of Zebedee and two other disciples were also there. Simon Peter said, 'I am going out fishing.' 'We will go with you', said the others. So they started and got into the boat. But that night they caught nothing.

Morning came, and there stood Jesus on the beach, but the disciples did not know that it was Jesus. He called out to them, 'Friends, have you caught anything?' They answered 'No.' He said, 'Shoot the net to starboard, and you will make a catch.' They did so, and found they could not haul the net aboard, there were so many fish in it. Then the disciple whom Jesus loved said to Peter, 'It is the Lord!' When Simon Peter heard that, he wrapped his coat about him (for he had stripped) and plunged into the sea. The rest of them came on in the boat, towing the net full of fish; for they were not far from land, only about a hundred yards.

When they came ashore, they saw a charcoal fire there, with fish laid on it, and some bread. Jesus said, 'Bring some of your catch.' Simon Peter went aboard and dragged the net to land, full of big fish, a hundred and fifty-three of them; and yet, many as they were, the net was not torn. Jesus said, 'Come and have breakfast.' None of the disciples dared to ask 'Who are you?' They knew it was the Lord. Jesus now came up, took the bread, and gave it to them, and the fish in the same way.

This makes the third time that Jesus appeared to his disciples after his resurrection from the dead.

After breakfast, Jesus said to Simon Peter, 'Simon son of John, do you love me more than all else?' 'Yes, Lord,' he answered, 'you know that I love you.' 'Then feed my lambs', he said. A second time he asked, 'Simon son of John, do you love me?' 'Yes, Lord, you know I love you.' 'Then tend my sheep.' A third time he said, 'Simon son of John, do you love me?' Peter was hurt that he asked him a third time, 'Do you love me?' 'Lord,' he said, 'you know everything; you know I love you.' Jesus said, 'Feed my sheep.'

'And further, I tell you this in very truth: when you were young you fastened your belt about you and walked where you chose; but when you are old you will stretch out your arms, and a stranger will bind you fast, and carry you where you have no wish to go.' He said this to indicate the manner of death by which Peter was to glorify God. Then he added, 'Follow me.'

Day 6

Despite repeated warnings by the Jewish leaders, and imprisonment, Peter continued to preach, and the Christian Church continued to grow. This reading tells of his imprisonment by Herod. Herod represents those people in power who persecute others for their beliefs. This has happened to a horrendous extent in our own century. Peter's faith and the power of prayer bring about his miraculous escape.

The Acts of the Apostles, chapter 12, verses 1–17

It was about this time that King Herod attacked certain members of the church. He beheaded James, the brother of John, and then, when he saw that the Jews approved, proceeded to arrest Peter also. This happened during the festival of Unleavened Bread. Having secured him, he put him in prison under a military guard, four squads of four men each, meaning to produce him in public after Passover. So Peter was kept in prison under constant watch, while the church kept praying fervently for him to God.

On the very night before Herod had planned to bring him forward, Peter was asleep between two soldiers, secured by two chains, while outside the doors sentries kept guard over the prison. All at once an angel of the Lord stood there, and the cell was ablaze with light. He tapped Peter on the shoulder and woke him. 'Quick! Get up', he said, and the chains fell away from his wrists. The angel then said to him, 'Do up your belt and put your sandals on.' He did so. 'Now wrap your cloak round you and follow me.' He followed him out, with no idea that the angel's intervention was real: he thought it was just a vision. But they passed the first guard-post, then the second, and reached the iron gate leading out into the city, which opened for them of its own accord. And so they came out and walked the length of one street; and the angel left him.

Then Peter came to himself. 'Now I know it is true,' he said; 'the Lord has sent his angel and rescued me from Herod's clutches and from all that the Jewish people were expecting.' When he realized how things stood, he made for the house of Mary, the mother of John Mark, where a large company was at prayer. He knocked at the outer door and a maid called Rhoda came to answer it. She recognized Peter's voice and was so overjoyed that instead of opening the door she ran in and announced that Peter was standing outside. 'You are crazy', they told her; but she insisted that it was so. Then they said, 'It must be his guardian angel.' Meanwhile Peter went on knocking, and when they opened the door and saw him, they were astounded. With a movement of the hand he signed to them to keep quiet, and told them how the Lord had brought him out of prison. 'Report this to James and the members of the church', he said. Then he left the house and went off elsewhere.

Day 7

This reading is thought to have been written by Peter when he was in Rome. He addressed it to the Christians who were scattered by persecution to various parts of the Middle East. He encourages them to consider carefully the quality of their lives now that they have been redeemed by Christ's dying for them.

The First Letter of St Peter, chapter 1, verses 1–2 and 13–25

Peter, a messenger of Jesus Christ, sends this letter to God's people now dispersed in Pontus, Galatia, Cappadocia, Asia and Bithynia, whom God the Father knew and chose long ago to be made holy by his Spirit, that they might obey Jesus Christ and be cleansed by his blood: may you know more and more of God's grace and peace.

So brace up your minds, and, as men who know what they are doing, rest the full weight of your hopes on the grace that will be yours when Jesus Christ reveals himself. Live as obedient children before God. Don't let your character be moulded by the desires of your ignorant days, but be holy in every part of your lives, for the one who has called you is himself holy. The scripture says:
Ye shall be holy; for I am holy.
If you pray to a Father who judges men by their actions without the slightest favouritism, then you should spend the time of your stay here on earth with reverent fear. For you must realize that you have been ransomed from the futile way of living passed on to you by your traditions, but not by any money payment of this passing world. No, the price was in fact the life-blood of Christ, the unblemished and unstained lamb of sacrifice. It is true that he was destined for this purpose before the world was founded, but it was for your benefit that he was revealed in these last days – for you who found your faith in God through him. And God raised him from the dead and gave him heavenly splendour, so that all your faith and hope might be centred in God.
Now that you have, by obeying the truth, made your souls clean enough for a genuine love of your fellows, see that you do love each other, fervently and from the heart. For you are not just mortals now

but sons of God; the live, permanent Word of the living God has given you his own indestructible heredity. It is true that:

> All flesh is as grass,
> And all the glory thereof as the flower of grass.
> The grass withereth, and the flower falleth:
> But the word of the Lord abideth for ever.

The Word referred to is the message of the gospel that was preached to you.

Day 8

This reading also comes from the first letter of St Peter to the Christians. Here he describes how those who work for others should be patient even when they are treated badly. He was writing to people who knew what it was to be persecuted for their faith.

The First Letter of St Peter, chapter 2, verses 18–25

You who are servants should submit to your masters with proper respect – not only to the good and kind, but also to the difficult. A man does a fine thing when he endures pain, with a clear conscience towards God, though he knows he is suffering unjustly. After all, it is no credit to you if you are patient in bearing a punishment which you have richly deserved! But if you do your duty and are punished for it and can still accept it patiently, you are doing something worthwhile in God's sight. Indeed this is your calling. For Christ suffered for you and left you a personal example, so that you might follow in his footsteps. He was guilty of no sin nor of the slightest prevarication. Yet when he was insulted he offered no insult in return. When he suffered he made no threats of revenge. He simply committed his cause to the One who judges fairly. And he personally bore our sins in his own body on the cross, so that we might be dead to sin and alive to all that is good. It was the suffering that he bore which has healed you. You had wandered away like so many sheep, but now you have returned to the shepherd and guardian of your souls.

◆

6

The early Christian Church

The Roman historian Tacitus, writing in the 1st century AD, mentions the crucifixion of a preacher in an obscure Roman colony called Judaea. Within 400 years the entire Roman Empire including North Africa, the Middle East and most of Europe had become Christian; and this happened at a time when people travelled on foot unless they could afford the fastest means of transport, travelling on horseback or by ship. The story of this transformation is a fascinating one and it begins with the stories of the resurrected Christ appearing to his disciples.

Day 1

This story of the resurrected Christ is about 'doubting Thomas'. He would not believe what he could not see with his own eyes. Jesus points out that faith requires a deeper understanding which does not need visual proof.

St John's Gospel, chapter 20, verses 19–29

Late that Sunday evening, when the disciples were together behind locked doors, for fear of the Jews, Jesus came and stood among them. 'Peace be with you!' he said, and then showed them his hands and his side. So when the disciples saw the Lord, they were filled with joy. Jesus repeated, 'Peace be with you!' and said, 'As the Father sent me, so I send you.' Then he breathed on them, saying, 'Receive the Holy Spirit! If you forgive any man's sins, they stand forgiven; if you pronounce them unforgiven, unforgiven they remain.'

One of the Twelve, Thomas, that is 'the Twin', was not with the rest when Jesus came. So the disciples told him, 'We have seen the Lord.' He said, 'Unless I see the mark of the nails on his hands, unless I put my finger into the place where the nails were, and my hand into his side, I will not believe it.'

A week later his disciples were again in the room, and Thomas was with them. Although the doors were locked, Jesus came and stood among them, saying, 'Peace be with you!' Then he said to Thomas, 'Reach your finger here; see my hands. Reach your hand here and put it into my side. Be unbelieving no longer, but believe.' Thomas said, 'My Lord and my God!' Jesus said, 'Because you have seen me you have found faith. Happy are they who never saw me and yet have found faith.'

Day 2

Before Jesus was crucified, he told his disciples that after he was dead he would send his Holy Spirit to inspire them. Then they would feel empowered to spread the Good News of his teaching to an ever wider public. With this teaching went a new understanding of the meaning of life, and a moral renewal.

It was on the Jewish festival of Pentecost that the disciples felt this Spirit.

The Acts of the Apostles, chapter 2, verses 1–8, 14, and 32–47

While the day of Pentecost was running its course they were all together in one place, when suddenly there came from the sky a noise like that of a strong driving wind, which filled the whole house where they were sitting. And there appeared to them tongues like flames of fire, dispersed among them and resting on each one. And they were all filled with the Holy Spirit and began to talk in other tongues, as the Spirit gave them power of utterance.

Now there were living in Jerusalem devout Jews drawn from every nation under heaven; and at this sound the crowd gathered, all bewildered because each one heard his own language spoken. They were amazed and in their astonishment exclaimed, 'Why, they are all Galileans, are they not, these men who are speaking? How is it then that we hear them, each of us in his own native language?

But Peter stood up with the Eleven, raised his voice, and addressed them: 'Fellow Jews, and all you who live in Jerusalem... 'The Jesus we speak of has been raised by God, as we can all bear witness. Exalted thus with God's right hand, he received the Holy Spirit from the Father, as was promised, and all that you now see and hear flows from him. Let all Israel then accept as certain that God has made this Jesus, whom you crucified, both Lord and Messiah.'

When they heard this they were cut to the heart, and said to Peter and the apostles, 'Friends, what are we to do?' 'Repent,' said Peter, 'repent and be baptized, every one of you, in the name of Jesus the Messiah for the forgiveness of your sins; and you will receive the gift of the Holy Spirit. For the promise is to you, and to your children, and to all who are far away, everyone whom the Lord our God may call.'

In these and many other words he pressed his case and pleaded with them: 'Save yourselves', he said, 'from this crooked age.' Then those who accepted his word were baptized, and some three thousand were added to their number that day.

They met constantly to hear the apostles teach, and to share the common life, to break bread, and to pray. A sense of awe was everywhere, and many marvels and signs were brought about through the apostles. All whose faith had drawn them together held everything in common: they would sell their property and possessions and make a general distribution as the need of each required. With one mind they kept up their daily attendance at the temple, and, breaking bread in private houses, shared their meals with unaffected joy, as they praised God and enjoyed the favour of the whole people. And day by day the Lord added to their number those whom he was saving.

Day 3

The disciples found that, having lived with Jesus and then been inspired by his Spirit, they had the power not only to preach but also to heal.

The Acts of the Apostles, chapter 3, verses 1–16

One day at three in the afternoon, the hour of prayer, Peter and John were on their way up to the temple. Now a man who had been a cripple from birth used to be carried there and laid every day by the gate of the temple called 'Beautiful Gate', to beg from people as they went in. When he saw Peter and John on their way into the temple he asked for charity. But Peter fixed his eyes on him, as John did also, and said, 'Look at us.' Expecting a gift from them, the man was all attention. And Peter said, 'I have no silver or gold; but what I have I give you: in the name of Jesus Christ of Nazareth, walk.' Then he grasped him by the right hand and pulled him up; and at once his feet and ankles grew strong; he sprang up, stood on his feet, and started to walk. He entered the temple with them, leaping and praising God, as he went. Everyone saw him walking and praising God, and when they recognized him as the man who used to sit begging at Beautiful Gate, they were filled with wonder and amazement at what had happened to him. And as he was clutching Peter and John all the people came running in astonishment towards them in Solomon's Portico, as it is called. Peter saw them coming and met them with these words: 'Men of Israel, why be surprised at this? Why stare at us as if we had made this man walk by some power or godliness of our own? The God of Abraham, Isaac, and Jacob, the God of our fathers, has given the highest honour to his servant Jesus, whom you committed for trial and repudiated in Pilate's court – repudiated the one who was holy and righteous when Pilate had decided to release him. You begged as a favour the release of a murderer, and killed him who has led the way to life. But God raised him from the dead; of that we are witnesses. And the name of Jesus, by awakening faith, has strengthened this man, whom you see and know, and this faith has made him completely well, as you can all see for yourselves.

Day 4

Like Jesus himself, the disciples suffered for their beliefs. It is though that eleven of the twelve original disciples eventually died at the hand. of those who felt their power threatened by this new religion.

One story of persecution is told in The Acts of the Apostles. It is particularly interesting because of the opinion expressed by the Pharisee called Gamaliel. He mentions other religious movements, all of which came to nothing. This is something that has happened throughout the centuries and that we experience in our own time. What Gamaliel said then has remained true: only those which are truly inspired by God survive.

The Acts of the Apostles, chapter 5, verses 27–42

So they brought them and stood them before the Council; and the High Priest began his examination. 'We expressly ordered you', he said, 'to desist from teaching in that name; and what has happened? You have filled Jerusalem with your teaching, and you are trying to make us responsible for that man's death.' Peter replied for himself and the apostles: 'We must obey God rather than men. The God of our fathers raised up Jesus whom you had done to death by hanging him on a gibbet. He it is whom God has exalted with his own right hand as leader and saviour, to grant Israel repentance and forgiveness of sins. And we are witnesses to all this, and so is the Holy Spirit given by God to those who are obedient to him.'

This touched them on the raw, and they wanted to put them to death. But a member of the Council rose to his feet, a Pharisee called Gamaliel, a teacher of the law held in high regard by all the people. He moved that the men be put outside for a while. Then he said, 'Men of Israel, be cautious in deciding what to do with these men. Some time ago Theudas came forward, claiming to be somebody, and a number of men, about four hundred, joined him. But he was killed and his whole following was broken up and disappeared. After him came Judas the Galilean at the time of the census; he induced some people to revolt under his leadership, but he too perished and his whole following was scattered. And so now: keep clear of these men, I tell you; leave them alone. For if this idea of theirs or its execution is of human origin, it will collapse; but if it is from God, you will never be able to put them down, and you risk finding yourselves at war with God.'

They took his advice. They sent for the apostles and had them flogged; then they ordered them to give up speaking in the name of Jesus, and discharged them. So the apostles went out from the Council rejoicing that they had been found worthy to suffer indignity for the sake of the Name. And every day they went steadily on with their teaching in the temple and in private houses, telling the good news of Jesus the Messiah.

Day 5

The first Christian to die for his faith was St Stephen. The way in which he forgave his persecutors before he died was such an inspiration that it drew many more to the faith. Another significant aspect of his story is that one of those persecutors was a man called Saul, later known as St Paul, who eventually became a Christian himself.

The Acts of the Apostles, chapter 6, verses 7–15, and chapter 7, verses 51–60

The word of God now spread more and more widely; the number of disciples in Jerusalem went on increasing rapidly, and very many of the priests adhered to the Faith.

Stephen, who was full of grace and power, began to work great miracles and signs among the people. But some members of the synagogue called the Synagogue of Freedmen, comprising Cyrenians and Alexandrians and people from Cilicia and Asia, came forward and argued with Stephen, but could not hold their own against the inspired wisdom with which he spoke. They then put up men who alleged that they had heard him make blasphemous statements against Moses and against God. They stirred up the people and the elders and doctors of the law, set upon him and seized him, and brought him before the Council. They produced false witnesses who said, 'This man is for ever saying things against this holy place and against the Law. For we have heard him say that Jesus of Nazareth will destroy this place and alter the customs handed down to us by Moses.' And all who were sitting in the Council fixed their eyes on him, and his face appeared to them like the face of an angel.

And he said, 'How stubborn you are, heathen still at heart and deaf to the truth! You always fight against the Holy Spirit. Like fathers, like sons. Was there ever a prophet whom your fathers did not persecute? They killed those who foretold the coming of the Righteous One and now you have betrayed him and murdered him, you who received the Law as God's angels gave it to you, and yet have not kept it.'

This touched them on the raw and they ground their teeth with fury. But Stephen, filled with the Holy Spirit, and gazing intently up to heaven, saw the glory of God, and Jesus standing at God's right hand. 'Look,' he said, 'there is a rift in the sky; I can see the Son of Man standing at God's right hand!' At this they gave a great shout and stopped their ears. Then they made one rush at him and, flinging him out of the city, set about stoning him. The witnesses laid their coats at the feet of a young man named Saul. So they stoned Stephen, and as they did so, he called out, 'Lord Jesus, receive my spirit.' Then he fell on his knees and cried aloud, 'Lord, do not hold this sin against them,' and with that he died.

Day 6

Saul, later called St Paul, persecuted the Christians. Perhaps partly inspired by the example of St Stephen and then by his own visionary experience, he did a U-turn. He had the courage to change his mind. It was he who then travelled far and wide to spread Christianity throughout the Roman Empire.

The Acts of the Apostles, chapter 9, verses 1–22

Meanwhile Saul was still breathing murderous threats against the disciples of the Lord. He went to the High Priest and applied for letters to the synagogues at Damascus authorising him to arrest anyone he found, men or women, who followed the new way, and bring them to Jerusalem. While he was still on the road and nearing Damascus, suddenly a light flashed from the sky all around him. He fell to the ground and heard a voice saying, 'Saul, Saul, why do you persecute me?' 'Tell me, Lord,' he said, 'who you are.' The voice answered, 'I am Jesus, whom you are persecuting. But get up and go into the city, and you will be told what you have to do.' Meanwhile the men who were travelling with him stood speechless; they heard the voice but could see no one. Saul got up from the ground, but when he opened his eyes he could not see; so they led him by the hand and brought him into Damascus. He was blind for three days, and took no food or drink.

There was a disciple in Damascus named Ananias. He had a vision in which he heard the voice of the Lord: 'Ananias!' 'Here I am, Lord', he answered. The Lord said to him, 'Go at once to Straight Street, to the house of Judas, and ask for a man from Tarsus named Saul. You will find him at prayer; he has had a vision of a man named Ananias coming in and laying his hands on him to restore his sight.' Ananias answered, 'Lord, I have often heard about this man and all the harm he has done to thy people in Jerusalem. And he is here with authority from the chief priests to arrest all who invoke thy name.' But the Lord said to him, 'You must go, for this man is my chosen instrument to bring my name before the nations and their kings, and before the people of Israel. I myself will show him all that he must go through for my name's sake.' So Ananias went. He entered the house, laid his hands on him and said, 'Saul, my brother, the Lord Jesus, who appeared to you on your way here, has sent me to you so that you may recover your sight, and be filled with the Holy Spirit.' And immediately it seemed that scales fell from his eyes, and he regained his sight. Thereupon he was baptized, and afterwards he took food and his strength returned.

He stayed some time with the disciples in Damascus. Soon he was proclaiming Jesus publicly in the synagogues: 'This', he said, 'is the Son of God.' All who heard were astounded. 'Is not this the man', they said, 'who was in Jerusalem trying to destroy those who invoke this name? Did he not come here for the sole purpose of arresting them and taking them to the chief priests?' But Saul grew more and more forceful, and silenced the Jews of Damascus with his cogent proofs that Jesus was the Messiah.

◆

Opposite is a poem by John Betjeman which he wrote in answer to a talk on the radio by Mrs Knight, a humanist, who was attacking Christianity and suggesting that morality without religion was quite enough for people to live by. This poem also explains the relevance of St Paul's conversion to us today.

'The Conversion of St Paul'
by John Betjeman

Now is the time when we recall
The sharp Conversion of St Paul.
Converted! Turned the wrong way round –
A man who seemed till then quite sound,
Keen on religion – very keen –
No-one, it seems, had ever been
So keen on persecuting those
Who said that Christ was God and chose
To die for this absurd belief
As Christ had died beside the thief.
Then in a sudden blinding light
Paul knew that Christ was God all right –
And very promptly lost his sight.
Poor Paul! They led him by the hand
He who had been so high and grand
A helpless blunderer, fasting, waiting,
Three days inside himself debating
In physical blindness: 'As it's true
That Christ is God and died for you,
Remember all the things you did
To keep His gospel message hid.
Remember how you helped them even
To throw the stones that murdered Stephen.
And do you think that you are strong
Enough to own that you were wrong!'
They must have been an awful time,
Those three long days repenting crime
Till Ananias came and Paul
Received his sight, and more than all
His former strength, and was baptized.
Saint Paul is often criticized
By modern people who're annoyed
At his conversion, saying Freud
Explains it all. But they omit
The really vital point of it,

Which isn't *how* it was achieved
But what it was that Paul believed.
He knew as certainly as we
Know you are you and I am me
That Christ was all He claimed to be.
What is conversion? Turning round
From chaos to a love profound.
And chaos too is an abyss
In which the only life is this.
Such a belief is quite all right
If you are sure like Mrs Knight
And think morality will do
For all the ills we're subject to.
But raise your eyes and see with Paul
An explanation of it all.
Injustice, cancer's cruel pain,
All suffering that seems in vain,
The vastness of the universe,
Creatures like centipedes and worse –
All part of an enormous plan
Which mortal eyes can never scan
And out of it came God to man.
Jesus is God and came to show
The world we live in here below
Is just an antechamber where
We for His Father's house prepare.
What is conversion? Not at all
For me the experience of St Paul,
No blinding light, a fitful glow
Is all the light of faith I know
Which sometimes goes completely out
And leaves me plunging round in doubt
Until I will myself to go
And worship in God's house below –
My parish Church – and even there
I find distractions everywhere.
What is Conversion? Turning round
To gaze upon a love profound.

For some of us see Jesus plain
And never once look back again,
And some of us have seen and known
And turned and gone away alone,
But most of us turn slow to see
The figure hanging on a tree
And stumble on and blindly grope
Upheld by intermittent hope.
God grant before we die we all
May see the light as did St Paul.

Day 7

Belief in Christianity was originally confined to a group of Jews. St Peter then had a vision which convinced him that it should be allowed to spread beyond the Jewish nation. He and St Paul were the two who laid the foundations for worldwide Christianity.

The Acts of the Apostles, chapter 10, verses 1–28 and 34

At Caesarea there was a man named Cornelius, a centurion in the Italian cohort, as it was called. He was a religious man, and he and his whole family joined in the worship of God. He gave generously to help the Jewish people, and was regular in his prayers to God. One day about three in the afternoon he had a vision in which he clearly saw an angel of God, who came into his room and said, 'Cornelius!' He stared at him in terror. 'What is it, my Lord?' he asked.

The angel said, 'Your prayers and acts of charity have gone up to heaven to speak for you before God. And now send to Joppa for a man named Simon, also called Peter: he is lodging with another Simon, a tanner, whose house is by the sea.' So when the angel who was speaking to him had gone, he summoned two of his servants and a military orderly who was a religious man, told them the whole story, and sent them to Joppa.

Next day, while they were still on their way and approaching the city, about noon Peter went up on the roof to pray. He grew hungry and wanted something to eat. While they were getting it ready, he fell into a trance. He saw a rift in the sky, and a thing coming down that looked like a great sheet of sail-cloth. It was slung by the four corners, and was being lowered to the ground. In it he saw creatures of every kind, whatever walks or crawls or flies. Then there was a voice which said to him, 'Up, Peter, kill and eat.' But Peter said, 'No, Lord, no: I have never eaten anything profane or unclean.' The voice came again a second time: 'It is not for you to call profane what God counts clean.' This happened three times; and then the thing was taken up again into the sky.

While Peter was still puzzling over the meaning of the vision he had seen, the messengers of Cornelius had been asking the way to Simon's house, and now arrived at the entrance. They called out and asked if Simon Peter was lodging there. But Peter was thinking over the vision, when the Spirit said to him, 'Some men are here looking for you; make haste and go downstairs. You may go with them without any misgiving, for it was I who sent them.' Peter came down to the men and said, 'You are looking for me? Here I am. What brings you here?' 'We are from the centurion Cornelius,' they replied, 'a good and religious man, acknowledged as such by the whole Jewish nation. He was directed by a holy angel to send for you to his house and to listen to what you have to say.' So Peter asked them in and gave them a night's lodging. Next day he set out with them, accompanied by some members of the congregation at Joppa.

The day after that, he arrived at Caesarea. Cornelius was expecting them and had called together his relatives and close friends. When Peter arrived, Cornelius came to meet him, and bowed to the ground in deep reverence. But Peter raised him to his feet and said, 'Stand up; I am a man like anyone else.' Still talking with him he went in and found a large gathering. He said to them, 'I need not tell you that a Jew is forbidden by his religion to visit or associate with a man of another race; yet God has shown me clearly that I must not call any man profane or unclean. That is why I came here without demur when you sent for me.

'I now see how true it is that God has no favourites, but that in every nation the man who is godfearing and does what is right is acceptable to him.'

7

Christian themes

Many of the readings in this section come from the letters sent to groups of Christians by early Christian leaders such as St Paul. In some cases passages or poems from other sources have been juxtaposed in order to extend or reinforce the themes.

Day 1

In this reading, St Paul writes to the Christians at Rome about the kind of life they should lead in their new faith. It is full of high ideals which we should aim for and which, if followed, would lead to joy in the individual, and to a civilized and peaceful society.

St Paul's Letter to the Romans, chapter 12, verses 9–21

Let us have no imitation Christian love. Let us have a genuine hatred for evil and a real devotion to good. Let us have real warm affection for one another as between brothers, and a willingness to let the other man have the credit. Let us not allow slackness to spoil our work and let us keep the fires of the spirit burning, as we do our work for the Lord. Base your happiness on your hope in Christ. When trials come endure them patiently; steadfastly maintain the habit of prayer. Give freely to fellow-Christians in want, never grudging a meal or a bed to those who need them. And as for those who try to make your life a misery, bless them. Don't curse, bless. Share the happiness of those who are happy, and the sorrow of those who are sad. Live in harmony with each other. Don't become snobbish but take a real interest in ordinary people. Don't become set in your own opinions. Don't pay back a bad turn by a bad turn, to anyone. See that your public behaviour is above criticism. As far as your responsibility goes, live at peace with everyone. Never take vengeance into your own hands, my dear friends: stand back and let God punish if he will. For it is written:

Vengeance belongeth unto me: I will recompense, saith the Lord. And it is also written:

If thine enemy hunger, feed him;

If he thirst, give him to drink:

For in so doing thou shalt heap coals of fire upon his head. Don't allow yourself to be overpowered by evil. Take the offensive – overpower evil with good!

Day 2

These readings are about the relationship between the individual and the group. Human beings are dependent on each other for service, love and support. For this to work, we all have to be different so that we can perform the various jobs which society requires. A society of only bricklayers could not function any more than a body which consisted only of eyes. We should therefore value each other's differences and be content with our own positions.

St Paul's Letter to the Corinthians, chapter 12, verses 12–18 and 21–22

As the human body, which has many parts, is a unity, and those parts, despite their multiplicity, constitute one single body, so it is with Christ. For we were all baptized by the one Spirit into one body, whether we were Jews, Greeks, slaves or free men, and we have all had experience of the same Spirit.

Now the body is not one part but many. If the foot should say, 'Because I am not a hand I don't belong to the body,' does that alter the fact that the foot *is* a part of the body? Or if the ear should say, 'Because I am not an eye I don't belong to the body,' does that mean that the ear really is no part of the body? After all, if the body were all one eye, for example, where would be the sense of hearing? Or if it were all one ear, where would be the sense of smell?

So that the eye cannot say to the hand, 'I don't need you!' nor, again, can the head say to the feet, 'I don't need you!'

◆

St Paul's Letter to the Romans, chapter 12, verses 3–8

Don't cherish exaggerated ideas of yourself or your importance, but try to have a sane estimate of your capabilities by the light of the faith that God has given to you all. For just as you have many members in one physical body and those members differ in their functions, so we, though many in number, compose one body in Christ and are all members to one another. Through the grace of God we have different gifts. If our gift is preaching, let us preach to the limit of our vision. If it is serving others let us concentrate on our service; if it is teaching let us give all we have to our teaching; and if our gift be the stimulating of the faith of others let us set ourselves to it. Let the man who is called to give, give freely; let the man in authority work with enthusiasm; and let the man who feels sympathy for his fellows in distress help them cheerfully.

◆

This idea is reinforced in the following fable.

'The Body and Its Members'
by Aesop

In former days there was a quarrel among the members of the human body. Each part professed itself to be indignant at being obliged to work for the Stomach, which remained idle and enjoyed the fruits of their labour. They one and all resolved to rebel, and to grant him supplies no longer, but to let him shift for himself as well as he could. The Hands protested that they would not lift up a finger to keep him from starving. The Mouth wished he might never speak again if he took in the least bit of nourishment for him as long as he lived. The Teeth said, May we be rotten if ever we chew a morsel for him for the future! This solemn league and covenant was kept as long as anything of that kind can be kept, which was until each of the rebel Members pined away to the skin and bone, and could hold out no longer. Then they found there was no doing without the Stomach, and that, as idle and insignificant as he seemed, he contributed as much to the maintenance and welfare of all the other parts, as they did to his.

Moral: None for themselves are born.

◆

The seventeenth-century poet and priest John Donne was ill in bed when he heard a funeral bell. This is what he wrote about it.

From Meditation
by John Donne

Perchance he for whom this bell tolls may be so ill, as that he knows not it tolls for him; and perchance I may think myself so much better than I am, as that they who are about me, and see my state, may have caused it to toll for me, and I know not that. The Church is Catholic, universal, so are all her actions; all that she does belongs to all. When she baptizes a child, that action concerns me; for that child is thereby connected to that Head which is my Head too, and engraffed into that body, whereof I am a member. And when she buries a man, that action concerns me. As therefore the bell that rings to a sermon, calls not upon the preacher only, but upon the congregation to come; so this bell calls us all; but how much more me, who am brought so near the door by this sickness. The bell doth toll for him that thinks it doth; and though it intermit again, yet from that minute, that that occasion wrought upon him, he is united to God. Who casts not up his eye to the sun when it rises? but who takes off his eye from a comet when that breaks out? Who bends not his ear to any bell, which upon any occasion rings? but who can remove it from that bell, which is passing a piece of himself out of this world? No man is an island, entire of itself; every man is a piece of the continent, a part of the main; if a clod be washed away by the sea, Europe is the less, as well as if a promontory were, as well as if a manor of thy friends or of thine own were. Any man's death diminishes me, because I am involved in mankind. And therefore never send to know for whom the bell tolls; it tolls for thee.

Day 3

This reading is the famous passage about love from St Paul.

St Paul's Letter to the Corinthians, chapter 13, verses 1–13

If I speak with the eloquence of men and of angels, but have no love, I become no more than blaring brass or crashing cymbal. If I have the gift of foretelling the future and hold in my mind not only all human knowledge but the very secrets of God, and if I also have that absolute faith which can move mountains, but have no love, I amount to nothing at all. If I dispose of all that I possess, yes, even if I give my own body to be burned, but have no love, I achieve precisely nothing.

This love of which I speak is slow to lose patience – it looks for a way of being constructive. It is not possessive: it is neither anxious to impress nor does it cherish inflated ideas of its own importance.

Love has good manners and does not pursue selfish advantage. It is not touchy. It does not keep account of evil or gloat over the wickedness of other people. On the contrary, it shares the joy of those who live by the truth.

Love knows no limit to its endurance, no end to its trust, no fading of its hope; it can outlast anything. Love never fails.

In this life we have three lasting qualities – faith, hope and love. But the greatest of them is love.

◆

Christians believe that we get our idea of what true love is from God himself as revealed in Jesus Christ. In the following poem, the poet expresses the inadequacy which many people feel before this high ideal. Our own love falls short but that of God never does.

'Love'
by George Herbert

Love bade me welcome; yet my soul drew back,
    Guilty of dust and sin.
But quick-ey'd Love, observing me grow slack
    From my first entrance in,
Drew nearer to me, sweetly questioning
    If I lack'd any thing.

'A guest', I answer'd 'worthy to be here.'
Love said, 'You shall be he.'
'I the unkind, ungrateful? Ah my dear,
I cannot look on thee.'
Love took my hand, and smiling did reply,
'Who made the eyes but I?'

'Truth Lord, but I have marr'd them; let my shame
Go where it doth deserve.'
'And know you not', says Love, 'who bore the blame?'
'You must sit down', says Love, 'and taste my meat.'
So I did sit and eat.

Day 4

The next readings are about death and resurrection. Parts of the first passage are read at funeral services.

St Paul's Letter to the Corinthians, chapter 15, verses 35–44 and 51–58

But perhaps someone will ask, 'How is the resurrection achieved? With what sort of body do the dead arrive?'

In your own experience you know that a seed does not germinate without itself 'dying'. When you sow a seed you do not sow the 'body' that will eventually be produced, but bare grain, of wheat, for example, or one of the other seeds. God gives the seed a 'body' according to his laws – a different 'body' to each kind of seed.

Then again, all flesh is not identical. There is a difference in the flesh of human beings, animals, birds and fish.

There are bodies which exist in the heavens, and bodies which exist in this world. The splendour of an earthly body is quite a different thing from the splendour of a heavenly body. The sun, the moon and the stars all have their own particular splendour; and one star differs from another in splendour.

There are illustrations here of the raising of the dead. The body is 'sown' in corruption; it is raised beyond the reach of corruption. It is 'sown' in dishonour; it is raised in splendour. It is sown in weakness; it is raised in power. It is sown a natural body; it is raised a spiritual body. As there is a natural body so will there be a spiritual body.

Listen, and I will tell you a secret. We shall not all die, but suddenly, in the twinkling of an eye, every one of us will be changed as the last trumpet sounds! For the trumpet will sound and the dead shall be raised beyond the reach of corruption, and we shall be changed. For this perishable nature of ours must be wrapped in imperishability, these bodies which are mortal must be wrapped in immortality. So when the perishable is lost in the imperishable, the mortal lost in the immortal, this scripture will come true:

Death is swallowed up in victory.

Where now, O death, is your victory; where now is your stinging power? It is sin which gives death its sting, and it is the Law which gives sin its power. All thanks to God, then, who gives us the victory over these things through our Lord Jesus Christ!

And so, brothers of mine, stand firm! Let nothing move you as you busy yourselves in the Lord's work. Be sure that nothing you do for him is ever lost or ever wasted.

◆

From By Herself and Her Friends
by Joyce Grenfell

If I should go before the rest of you
Break not a flower nor inscribe a stone
Nor when I'm gone speak in a Sunday voice
But be the usual selves I have known
Weep if you want
Parting is hell
But life goes on
So sing as well.

◆

'The Next Room'
by Canon Henry Scott Holland

Death is nothing at all.

I have only slipped away into the next room.

I am I, You are You.

Whatever we were to each other, that we still are,

Call me by my own familiar name,

Speak to me in the easy way which you always used,

Put no difference in your tone, wear no forced air of solemnity or
sorrow.

Laugh as we always laughed at the little jokes we enjoyed together.

Pray, Smile, Think of me – Let my name be ever the household
word

that it always was.

Let it be spoken, without the trace of a shadow on it.

Life means all that it ever meant.

It is the same that it ever was, there is unbroken continuity.

Why should I be out of mind because I am out of sight?

Very near, just around the corner.

All is well.

Day 5

*These two readings are about ideals of moral behaviour which all
should aim to reach.*

*St Paul's Letter to the Ephesians, chapter 4,
verses 24–32, and chapter 5, verses 1–2*

You must be made new in mind and spirit, and put on the new
nature of God's creating, which shows itself in the just and devout
life called for by the truth.

Then throw off falsehood; speak the truth to each other.

If you are angry, do not let anger lead you into sin; do not let sunset find you still nursing it; leave no loop-hole for the devil.

The thief must give up stealing, and instead work hard and honestly with his own hands, so that he may have something to share
with the needy.

No bad language must pass your lips, but only what is good and helpful to the occasion, so that it brings a blessing to those who hear it. And do not grieve the Holy Spirit of God.

Have done with spite and passion, all angry shouting and cursing, and bad feeling of every kind.

Be generous to one another, tender-hearted, forgiving one another as God in Christ forgave you.

In a word, as God's dear children, try to be like him, and live in love as Christ loved you, and gave himself up on your behalf as an offering and sacrifice whose fragrance is pleasing to God.

♦

St Paul ends his letter to the Ephesians with this picture of the Christian as he or she faces the struggle between good and evil.

St Paul's Letter to the Ephesians, chapter 6, verses 10–18

In conclusion be strong – not in yourselves but in the Lord, in the power of his boundless strength. Put on God's complete armour so that you can successfully resist all the devil's craftiness. For our fight is not against any physical enemy: it is against organizations and powers that are spiritual. We are up against the unseen power that controls this dark world, and spiritual agents from the very headquarters of evil. Therefore you must wear the whole armour of God that you may be able to resist evil in its day of power, and that even when you have fought to a standstill you may still stand your ground. Take your stand then with truth as your belt, integrity your breastplate, the gospel of peace firmly on your feet, salvation as your helmet and in your hand the sword of the Spirit, the Word of God. Above all be sure you take faith as your shield, for it can quench every burning missile the enemy hurls at you. In all your petitions pray at all times with every kind of spiritual prayer, keeping alert and persistent as you pray for all Christ's men and women.

Day 6

In this passage, Paul is advising Timothy on how to deal with the Church at Ephesus, who rely too much on the riches of this world.

St Paul's First Letter to Timothy, chapter 6, verses 7–10 and 17–19

We brought nothing with us when we entered this world and we can be sure we shall take nothing with us when we leave it. Surely then, as far as physical things are concerned, it is sufficient for us to keep our bodies fed and clothed. For men who set their hearts on being wealthy expose themselves to temptation. They fall into a trap and lay themselves open to all sorts of silly and wicked desires, which are quite capable of utterly ruining and destroying their souls. For loving money leads to all kinds of evil, and some men in the struggle to be rich have lost their faith and caused themselves untold agonies of mind.

Tell those who are rich in this present world not to be contemptuous of others, and not to rest the weight of their confidence on the transitory power of wealth but on the living God, who generously gives us everything for our enjoyment. Tell them to do good, to be rich in kindly actions, to be ready to give to others and to sympathize with those in distress. Their security should be invested in the life to come, so that they may be sure of holding a share in the life which is real and permanent.

8
The teachings of Jesus

◆

The readings in this chapter could be used as a sequence. The thread running through them is Jesus's Sermon on the Mount. The first reading consists of the opening part of this sermon and then each of the declarations in it is taken separately and explained or exemplified by other readings, some from the Bible and some from other sources.

Day 1

This reading is the first part of what is called the Sermon on the Mount. It is called this because Jesus positioned himself on a hill so that the people could hear him. In the Sermon Jesus describes those qualities of character which make a person deeply happy or 'blest'.

St Matthew's Gospel, chapter 5, verses 1–12

When he saw the crowds he went up the hill. There he took his seat, and when his disciples had gathered round him he began to address them. And this is the teaching he gave:
'How blest are those who know their need of God;
the kingdom of Heaven is theirs.
How blest are the sorrowful;
they shall find consolation.
How blest are those of a gentle spirit;
They shall have the earth for their possession.
How blest are those who hunger and thirst to see right prevail;
they shall be satisfied.
How blest are those who show mercy;
mercy shall be shown to them.
How blest are those whose hearts are pure;
they shall see God.
How blest are the peacemakers;
God shall call them his sons.

How blest are those who have suffered persecution for the cause of right; the kingdom of Heaven is theirs.

How blest you are, when you suffer insults and persecution and every kind of calumny for my sake. Accept it with gladness and exultation, for you have a rich reward in heaven; in the same way they persecuted the prophets before you.'

Day 2

The first quality of character described by Jesus in his Sermon on the Mount is expressed in these words: 'How blest are those who know their need of God; the kingdom of Heaven is theirs.' There is a story which illustrates just this point. An arrogant person is not a happy one; but a person who knows their own need for something greater than themselves is more likely to gain peace and joy.

The story is from St Luke's Gospel. Pharisees were important religious leaders; tax-gatherers were unpopular and sometimes corrupt.

St Luke's Gospel, chapter 18, verses 9–14

And here is another parable that he told. It was aimed at those who were sure of their own goodness and looked down on everyone else. 'Two men went up to the temple to pray, one a Pharisee and the other a tax-gatherer. The Pharisee stood up and prayed thus: "I thank thee, O God, that I am not like the rest of men, greedy, dishonest, adulterous; or, for that matter, like this tax-gatherer. I fast twice a week; I pay tithes on all that I get." But the other kept his distance and would not even raise his eyes to heaven, but beat upon his breast, saying, "O God, have mercy on me, sinner that I am." It was this man, I tell you, and not the other, who went home acquitted of his sins. For everyone who exalts himself will be humbled; and whoever humbles himself will be exalted.'

◆

The next passage is also about the Christian belief of our need for God, but the writer addresses himself particularly to young people. He suggests that it is important to search for God while still young so that when we need him he is familiar to us. The series of pictures he gives to describe old age and its declining powers emphasizes how difficult it is to begin looking for God when our faculties no longer have their energy or strength.

Book of Ecclesiastes, chapter 12, verses 1–7

Remember your Creator in the days of your youth, before the time of trouble comes and the years draw near when you will say, 'I see no purpose in them.' Remember him before the sun and the light of day give place to darkness, before the moon and the stars grow dim, and the clouds return with the rain – when the guardians of the house tremble, and the strong men stoop, when the women grinding the meal cease work because they are few, and those who look through the windows look no longer, when the street-doors are shut, when the noise of the mill is low, when the chirping of the sparrow grows faint, and the song-birds fall silent; when men are afraid of a steep place and the street is full of terrors, when the blossom whitens on the almond-tree and the locust's paunch is swollen and caper-buds have no more zest. For man goes to his everlasting home, and the mourners go about the streets. Remember him before the silver cord is snapped and the golden bowl is broken, before the pitcher is shattered at the spring and the wheel broken at the well, before the dust returns to the earth as it began and the spirit returns to God who gave it.

Day 3

It seems strange to say 'How blest are the sorrowful'. How can anyone be happy and sad at the same time? But Jesus, in this second saying about the happy character, goes on to say, 'they shall find consolation'. Sometimes, when a little child is hurt, it finds such comfort in its mother's arms that it is almost glad to have fallen. Jesus suggests that the comfort of God may be a joy even at times of sorrow.

The following passages are about the comfort of God.

Book of Isaiah, chapter 61, verses 1–3, and chapter 66, verse 13

> The spirit of the Lord God is upon me
> because the Lord has anointed me;
> he has sent me to bring good news to the humble,
> to bind up the broken-hearted,
> to proclaim liberty to captives
> and release to those in prison;
> to proclaim a year of the Lord's favour
> and a day of the vengeance of our God;
> to comfort all who mourn,
> to give them garlands instead of ashes,
> oil of gladness instead of mourners' tears,
> a garment of splendour for the heavy heart.
>
> As a mother comforts her son,
> so will I myself comfort you,
> and you shall find comfort in Jerusalem.

St Matthew's Gospel, chapter 11, verses 28–30

Jesus said:

'Come to me, all whose work is hard, whose load is heavy; and I will give you relief. Bend your necks to my yoke, and learn from me, for I am gentle and humble-hearted; and your souls will find relief. For my yoke is good to bear, my load is light.'

♦

'n this third reading God spoke these words to Joshua as the people of 'srael were just about to cross the Jordan to the Promised Land.

Book of Joshua, chapter 1, verse 9

Have I not commanded you? Be strong and of good courage; be not 'rightened, neither be dismayed; for the Lord your God is with you wherever you go.

♦

The fourth reading is an anonymous passage.

'Footprints'

One night I had a dream.

I dreamed I was walking along the beach with God and across the sky flashed scenes from my life. For each scene I noticed two sets of footprints in the sand, one belonged to me and the other to God.

When the last scene of my life flashed before me I looked back at the footprints in the sand. I noticed that at times along the path of life there was only one set of footprints.

I also noticed that it happened at the very lowest and saddest times of my life. This really bothered me and I questioned God about it.

'God, You said that once I decided to follow You, You would walk with me all the way but I noticed that during the most troublesome time in my life there is only one set of footprints. I don't understand why in times when I needed You most, You would leave me.'

God replied, 'My precious, precious child, I love you and I would never, never leave you during your times of trials and suffering. When you see only one set of footprints it was then that I carried you.'

Day 4

The following reading concerns this verse from the Sermon on the Mount: 'How blest are those of a gentle spirit; they shall have the earth for their possession.'

In this passage the Russian writer Tolstoy argues that gentleness and not violence is more natural to human beings.

From What I Believe
by Tolstoy

The least one can demand of people who judge any doctrine is that they should judge of it in the sense in which the teacher himself understood it. And Christ understood his teaching not as a distant ideal for humanity, obedience to which is impossible, nor as a mystical poetic fantasy wherewith he captivated the simple-minded inhabitants of Galilee. He understood his teaching as a real thing, and a thing which would save mankind. And he did not dream on the cross but died for his teaching, and many others are dying and will yet die. Of such a teaching one cannot say that it is a dream!

Every true doctrine is a dream to those in error. We have come to this, that there are many people (of whom I was one) who say that this teaching is visionary because it is not natural to man. It is not in accord, they say, with man's nature to turn the other cheek when one cheek is struck; it is not natural to give what is one's own to another; it is unnatural to work for others instead of for oneself. It is natural to man, they say, to defend his safety and the safety of his family and his property: in other words, it is natural for man to struggle for his own existence. The learned jurists prove scientifically that man's most sacred duty is to defend his rights, that is – to struggle.

But it is sufficient to free oneself for a moment from the thought that the order which exists and has been arranged by men is the best and is sacrosanct, for the objection that Christ's teaching is not accordant with man's nature to turn against the objector. Who will deny that to murder or torture, I will not say a man, but to torture a dog or kill a hen or calf is contrary and distressing to man's nature? (I know people who live by tilling the land, and who have given up eating meat merely because they had themselves to kill their own animals.) Yet the whole structure of our lives is such that each man's personal advantage is obtained by inflicting suffering on others, which is contrary to human nature. The whole order of our life and the whole complex mechanism of our institutions, designed for the infliction of violence, witness to the extent to which violence is contrary to human nature. Not a single judge would decide to strangle with a rope the man he condemns to death from the bench. Not a single magistrate would make up his mind himself to take a peasant from his weeping family and shut him up in prison. None of our generals or soldiers, were it not for discipline, oaths of allegiance, and declarations of war, would, will not say kill hundreds of Turks and Germans and destroy their villages, but even wound a single man. All this is only done thanks to a very complex state and social machinery the purpose of which is so to distribute the responsibility for the evil deeds that are done that no one should feel the unnaturalness of those deeds. Some men write the laws; others apply them; a third set drill men and habituate them to discipline, that is to say, to senseless and implicit obedience; a fourth set – the people who are disciplined – commit all sorts of deeds of violence, even killing people, without knowing why or wherefore. But a man need only, even for a moment, free himself mentally from this net of worldly organization in which he is involved to understand what is really unnatural to him.

Day 5

The next statement from the Sermon on the Mount is, 'How blest are those who hunger and thirst to see right prevail; they shall be satisfied.'

The following passage, which comes from later in the Sermon, does not at first seem related to it. The subject is the importance of not relying on material things. It is also about priorities in life, about putting what is right and just before our own gain.

St Matthew's Gospel, chapter 6, verses 19–34

Do not store up for yourselves treasure on earth, where it grows rusty and moth-eaten, and thieves break in to steal it. Store up treasure in heaven, where there is no moth and no rust to spoil it, no thieves to break in and steal. For where your treasure is, there will your heart be also.

'No servant can be slave to two masters; for either he will hate the first and love the second, or he will be devoted to the first and think nothing of the second. You cannot serve God and Money.

'Therefore I bid you put away anxious thoughts about food and drink to keep you alive, and clothes to cover your body. Surely life is more than food, the body more than clothes. Look at the birds of the air; they do not sow and reap and store in barns, yet your heavenly Father feeds them. You are worth more than the birds! Is there a man of you who by anxious thought can add a foot to his height? And why be anxious about clothes? Consider how the lilies grow in the fields; they do not work, they do not spin; and yet, I tell you, even Solomon in all his splendour was not attired like one of these. But if that is how God clothes the grass in the fields, which is there today, and tomorrow is thrown on the stove, will he not all the more clothe you? How little faith you have! No, do not ask anxiously, "What are we to eat? What are we to drink? What shall we wear?" All these are things for the heathen to run after, not for you, because your heavenly Father knows that you need them all. Set your mind on God's kingdom and his justice before everything else, and all the rest will come to you as well. So do not be anxious about tomorrow; tomorrow will look after itself. Each day has troubles enough of its own.'

Day 6

The next words in the Sermon on the Mount are: 'How blest are those who show mercy; mercy shall be shown to them.'

The same theme is to be found in this medieval prayer:

'Those who have sinned against us or we against them'
by Thomas à Kempis

We offer unto Thee our prayers and intercessions, for those especially who have in any matter hurt, grieved or found fault with us or who have done us any damage or displeasure.

For all those also whom, at any time, we have vexed, troubled, burdened, and scandalized, by words or deeds, knowingly or in ignorance: that Thou wouldst grant us all equally pardon for our sins, and for our offences against each other.

Take away from our hearts, O Lord, all suspiciousness, indigna-
tion, wrath and contention, and whatsoever may hurt charity, and
lessen brotherly love. Have mercy, O Lord, have mercy on those that
crave thy mercy, give grace unto them that stand in need thereof,
and make us such that we may be worthy to enjoy Thy grace, and
go forward to life eternal.

♦

*This is a fable about the futility of anger. It is commented on by
G F Townsend.*

'The Wind and the Sun'
by Aesop

A dispute once arose betwixt the North Wind and the Sun about the
superiority of their power; and they agreed to try their strength upon
a traveller, which should be able to get his cloak off first. The North
Wind began, and blew a very cold blast, accompanied with a sharp,
driving shower. But this, and whatever else he could do, instead of
making the man quit his cloak, obliged him to gird it about his body
as close as possible. Next came the Sun; who, breaking out from a
thick watery cloud, drove away the cold vapours from the sky, and
darted his warm, sultry beams upon the head of the poor weather-
beaten traveller. The man growing faint with the heat, and unable to
endure it any longer, first throws off his heavy cloak, and then flies
for protection to the shade of a neighbouring grove.

Moral: A soft tongue breaketh the bone.

Application: How much more powerful a motive in human
actions is love than fear! How much more readily does the heart of
the man or of the child respond to kindness than to harshness! There
is a very remarkable reflection attributed to the Emperor Napoleon,
when, as an exile at St Helena, he looked back on his past life. He
is reported to have said, 'My empire, and those of the other great
conquerors, Alexander the Great, Caesar, Charlemagne, were all
founded on fear; and all have perished. There was only one based
on love, that of the Great Author of Christianity; and that alone continues, and will endure.' The spirit of the Master should animate His
followers. The law of kindness finds the greatest access to the human
heart. Persuasion prevails more than force. Mildness governs more
than anger. Fair and soft go far in a day.

Seek not with violence to do
What patience may effect;
By gentle means, 'tis easier oft
To heal and to correct.

Loud threatenings make men stubborn, but kind words
Pierce gentle breasts sooner than sharpest swords.

Day 7

*We now consider this verse from the Sermon on the Mount: 'How bless
are those whose hearts are pure; they shall see God'; and illustrate i
with some verses from St Matthew's Gospel.*

*St Matthew's Gospel, chapter 19,
verses 13–15, and chapter 18, verses 1–7 and verse 10*

They brought children for him to lay his hands on them with
prayer. The disciples rebuked them, but Jesus said to them, 'Let the
children come to me; do not try to stop them; for the kingdom o
Heaven belongs to such as these.' And he laid his hands on the
children, and went his way.

At that time the disciples came to Jesus and asked, 'Who is the great
est in the kingdom of Heaven?' He called a child, set him in front o
them, and said,

'I tell you this: unless you turn round and become like children
you will never enter the kingdom of Heaven. Let a man humble him
self till he is like this child, and he will be the greatest in the kingdom
of Heaven. Whoever receives one such child in my name receives
me.

'Never despise one of these little ones; I tell you, they have thei
guardian angels in heaven, who look continually on the face of my
heavenly Father.'

♦

The following two passages are taken from writings by Thomas Traherne, a seventeenth-century Christian mystic. Here he remembers with what rapture he looked out on the world when he was a little child. This joy is characteristic of those who are pure in heart.

From Centuries of Meditation
by Thomas Traherne

Your enjoyment of the World is never right, till you so esteem it, that everything in it, is more your treasure than a King's exchequer full of Gold and Silver. And that exchequer yours also in its place and service. Can you take too much joy in your Father's works? He is himself in everything. Some things are little on the outside, and rough and common, but I remember the time when the dust of the streets were as precious as Gold to my infant eyes, and now they are more precious to the eye of reason.

Your enjoyment of the world is never right, till every morning you awake in Heaven; see yourself in your Father's Palace; and look upon the skies, the earth, and the air as Celestial Joys: having such a reverend esteem of all, as if you were among the Angels.

You never enjoy the world aright, till the Sea itself floweth in your veins, till you are clothed with the heavens, and crowned with the stars: and perceive yourself to be the sole heir of the whole world, and more than so, because men are in it who are every one sole heirs as well as you. Till you can sing and rejoice and delight in God, as misers do in gold, and Kings in sceptres, you never enjoy the world.

Till your spirit filleth the whole world, and the stars are your jewels; till you are as familiar with the ways of God in all Ages as with your walk and table: till you are intimately acquainted with that shady nothing out of which the world was made: till you love men so as to desire their happiness, with a thirst equal to the zeal of your own; till you delight in God for being good to all: you never enjoy the world.

It was His wisdom made you need the sun. It was His goodness made you need the sea. Be sensible of what you need, or enjoy neither. Consider how much you need them. For thence they derive their value. Suppose the sun were extinguished; or the sea were dry. There would be no light, no beauty, no warmth, no fruits, no flow ers, no pleasant gardens, feasts, or prospects. No wine no oil no bread, no life, no motion. Would you not give all the gold and silver in the Indies for such a treasure? Prize it now you have it, at that rate and you shall be a grateful creature; nay you shall be a divine and heavenly person. For they in heaven do prize blessings when they have them. They in earth when they have them prize them not; they in hell prize them, when they have them not.

♦

In this poem, the writer considers the traumas that face a baby com ing into the world. As it grows, it will not just be the victim of horror that people inflict upon each other but also the perpetrator. The baby will be sinned against but also be a sinner.

'Prayer Before Birth'
by Louis MacNeice

I am not yet born; O hear me.
Let not the bloodsucking bat or the rat or the stoat or the
club-footed ghoul come near me.

I am not yet born; console me.
I fear that the human race may with tall walls wall me,
with strong drugs dope me, with wise lies lure me,
on black racks rack me, in blood-baths roll me.

I am not yet born; provide me
With water to dandle me, grass to grow for me, trees to talk
to me, sky to sing to me, birds and a white light
in the back of my mind to guide me.

I am not yet born; forgive me
For the sins that in me the world shall commit, my words
when they speak me, my thoughts when they think me,
my treason engendered by traitors beyond me,
my life when they murder by means of my
hands, my death when they live me.

I am not yet born; rehearse me
In the parts I must play and the cues I must take when
old men lecture me, bureaucrats hector me, mountains
frown at me, lovers laugh at me, the white
waves call me to folly and the desert calls
me to doom and the beggar refuses
my gift and my children curse me.

I am not yet born; O hear me,
Let not the man who is beast or who thinks he is God
come near me.

I am not yet born; O fill me
With strength against those who would freeze my
humanity, would dragoon me into a lethal automaton,
would make me a cog in a machine, a thing with
one face, a thing, and against all those
who would dissipate my entirety, would
blow me like thistledown hither and
thither or hither and thither
like water held in the
hands would spill me.

Let them not make me a stone and let them not spill me.
Otherwise kill me.

Day 8

*This passage illustrates the words: 'How blest are the peacemakers;
God shall call them his sons.'*

St Paul's Letter to the Romans, chapter 12, verses 17–21

Never pay back evil for evil. Let your aims be such as all men count
honourable. If possible, so far as it lies with you, live at peace with
all men. My dear friends, do not seek revenge, but leave a place for
divine retribution; for there is a text which reads, 'Justice is mine,
says the Lord, I will repay.' But there is another text: 'If your enemy
is hungry, feed him; if he is thirsty, give him a drink; by doing this
you will heap live coals on his head.' Do not let evil conquer you,
but use good to defeat evil.

♦

In order to be a peacemaker, one has to know who the enemy is. The writer of the following passage is in the midst of terrible suffering, having spent two years imprisoned in Buchenwald Concentration Camp. Here he looks for the source of evil.

'The Real Enemy Is Within'
by Pierre d'Harcourt

This for me is the first lesson of the camp – that it made beasts of some men and saints of others. And the second lesson of the camp is that it is hard to predict who will be the saint and who the beast when the time of trial comes.

Men famous and honoured in pre-war France, regarded as natural leaders, showed neither spirit nor authority in the camp. Other men, of seemingly mediocre brains and character, who would never have been noticed in ordinary times, shone out like beacons as the true leaders. Under the stresses and strains imposed by life in the camp, only one thing prevailed – strength of character. Cleverness, creativeness, learning, all went down; only real goodness survived.

Sooner or later weakness of fibre was revealed in a man, and sooner or later it destroyed him. Self-discipline was essential, and this is the basis of character. For instance – the question of the open fire. It had been very tempting, especially in the cold winter nights, to go and lie by the open braziers in our blockhouse. But it was fatal. A man began by lying some distance from the fire, on the outer ring. But the fire drew like a magnet. He would go closer to the flames, until finally he would get as near as he possibly could. The contrast between the heat of the fire at night and the cold of the roll call in the morning was too much for these poor human frames. It was only a matter of time before it killed them.

The fact that every prisoner knew this did not prevent a great many from succumbing. If a prisoner began habitually to leave his bunk in the night and lie down to sleep on the floor around the fire, you knew that he had decided, even if he had not faced his own decision, that death was preferable to discomfort.

As I write about the temptation of the fire, which symbolizes all the temptations of the camp, I think of P., a famous scientist who was among us. P. had begun the downhill path by selling his margarine ration to obtain cigarettes. He could not afford this deficiency in fat, as he well knew, and it became necessary for him to obtain heat from the fire. Gradually P. moved from the outside circle of the sleepers to the centre. Every night he got a little nearer. For a week or so he slept as close to it as he could get. And then, because he had failed to discipline his craving for cigarettes, he died.

It seemed to me that those men displayed most character who had the capacity for living on their own and that these men possessed something which is easiest described as religion, faith, or devotion. I saw that leadership exercised by Christians. I saw it in communists, too. It was displayed by people who had no religious faith or political creed in any formal sense, but who still had some inner core which gave them a belief in life, when the rest of us were lost.

The camp showed me that a man's real enemies are not ranged against him along the borders of a hostile country; they are often among his own people – indeed, within his own mind. The worst enemies are hate and greed, and cruelty. The real enemy is within.

◆

This reading is from the last part of the Sermon on the Mount.

St Matthew's Gospel, chapter 7, verses 1–5

Pass no judgement, and you will not be judged. For as you judge others, so you will yourselves be judged, and whatever measure you deal out to others will be dealt back to you. Why do you look at the speck of sawdust in your brother's eye, with never a thought for the great plank in your own? Or how can you say to your brother, 'Let me take the speck out of your eye', when all the time there is that plank in your own? You hypocrite! First take the plank out of your own eye, and then you will see clearly to take the speck out of your brother's.

Day 9

In the Sermon on the Mount, Jesus says: 'How blest are those who have suffered persecution for the cause of right; the kingdom of Heaven is theirs.' This of course happened to Jesus himself on the cross on Good Friday.

In the following passage the author writes about Oscar Romero, a priest in El Salvador, a country where poverty and injustice were part of the system under a tyrannical government.

From Good Friday People
by Sheila Cassidy

Oscar Arnulfo Romero was named Archbishop of San Salvador on 28 February 1977. He was a quiet man, an introvert who believed that prayer and personal conversion were what mattered and who liked to keep his distance from the more revolutionary members of his flock. Little by little, however, he found himself drawn into the struggle of his people until he could declare in public,

'I am a shepherd who, with his people, has begun to learn a beautiful and difficult truth; our Christian faith requires that we submerge ourselves in this world. The world that the Church must serve is the world of the poor, and the poor are the ones who decide what it means for the Church to really live in the world.'

It was the poor who showed the Archbishop what they required of their church, not just the catechism and the sacraments but something much harder: to speak out against injustice, to be the voice of a people who had no voice. So that is what he did; week by week and month by month his sermons were broadcast to the nation and he denounced the killings, endemic among his people. In 1980 he received the Nobel Prize for Peace.

Later that year, Oscar Romero was assassinated by a government agent at the altar of his cathedral.

◆

This reading is the final passage from the Sermon on the Mount.

St Matthew's Gospel, chapter 7, verses 21–29

'Not everyone who calls me "Lord, Lord" will enter the kingdom of Heaven, but only those who do the will of my heavenly Father. When that day comes, many will say to me, "Lord, Lord, did we not prophesy in your name, cast out devils in your name, and in your name perform many miracles?" Then I will tell them to their face, "I never knew you: out of my sight, you and your wicked ways!"

'What then of the man who hears these words of mine and acts upon them? He is like a man who had the sense to build his house on rock. The rain came down, the floods rose, the wind blew, and beat upon that house; but it did not fall, because its foundations were on rock. But what of the man who hears these words of mine and does not act upon them? He is like a man who was foolish enough to build his house on sand. The rain came down, the floods rose, the wind blew, and beat upon that house; down it fell with a great crash.'

When Jesus had finished this discourse the people were astounded at his teaching; unlike their own teachers he taught with a note of authority.

9
The Ten Commandments

These readings could be used as a series, perhaps once a week for a term. Alternatively they could provide occasional passages to illustrate other subjects.

Day 1

The theme of these readings is the Ten Commandments. These were the laws which God gave to Moses on Mount Sinai.

These are the first two Commandments.

Book of Exodus, chapter 20, verses 1–6

God spoke, and these were his words: I am the Lord your God who brought you out of Egypt, out of the land of slavery.

You shall have no other god to set against me.

You shall not make a carved image for yourself nor the likeness of anything in the heavens above, or on the earth below, or in the waters under the earth.

You shall not bow down to them or worship them; for I, the Lord your God, am a jealous God. I punish the children for the sins of their fathers to the third and fourth generations of those who hate me. But I keep faith with thousands, with those who love me and keep my commandments.

In the next reading, Christ describes the things which people worship instead of worshipping God.

St Matthew's Gospel, chapter 6, verses 19–21

'Do not store up for yourselves treasure on earth, where it grows rusty and moth-eaten, and thieves break in to steal it. Store up treasure in heaven, where there is no moth and no rust to spoil it, no thieves to break in and steal. For where your treasure is, there will your heart be also.'

◆

The following words by Rabbi Gryn, who was President of the Reform Synagogues of Great Britain, were about his experiences in Auschwitz concentration camp.

'All sorts of things happened to my faith during the Holocaust and although I could not have articulated it in this way, there is one thing that I understood very precisely: what happened to us was not because of what God did but what people did after rejecting Him. I witnessed the destruction that follows when men try to turn themselves into gods.'

◆

The next story shows clearly the uses of wealth.

King Midas: The King with the Golden Touch

The god Bacchus granted King Midas the right to choose himself a gift – a privilege which Midas welcomed, but one which did him little good, for he was fated to make poor use of the opportunity he was given. He said to the god: 'Grant that whatever my person touches be turned to yellow gold.' Bacchus, though sorry that Midas had not asked for something better, granted his request, and presented him with this life-destroying gift.

The king went off cheerfully, delighted with the fortune which had befallen him. He tested the good faith of Bacchus' promise by touching this and that, and could scarcely believe his own senses when he broke a green twig from a low-growing branch of oak, and the twig turned to gold. He lifted a stone from the ground and the stone, likewise, gleamed pale gold. He touched a sod of earth and the earth, by the power of his touch, became a lump of ore. If he laid his finger on the pillars of his lofty doorways, they were seen to shine and glitter, and even when he washed his hands in clear water, the trickles that flowed over his palms became a golden shower. He dreamed of everything turned to gold, and his hopes soared beyond the limits of his imagination.

So he exulted in his good fortune, while servants set before him tables piled high with meats, and with bread in abundance. But then, when he touched a piece of bread, it grew stiff and hard: if he hungrily tried to bite into the meat, a sheet of gold encased the food, as soon as his teeth came in contact with it.

Wretched in spite of his riches, dismayed by the strange disaster which had befallen him, Midas prayed for a way of escape from his wealth, loathing what he had lately desired. No amount of food could relieve his hunger, parching thirst burned his throat, and he was tortured, as he deserved, by the gold he now hated.

Raising his shining arms, he stretched his hands to heaven and cried: 'Forgive me, father Bacchus! I have sinned, yet pity me, I pray, and save me speedily from this disaster that promised so fair!'

The gods are kind: when Midas confessed his fault, Bacchus restored him to his former state, cancelling the gift which, in fulfilment of his promise, he had given the king.

Day 2

This is the third Commandment.

Book of Exodus, chapter 20, verse 7

You shall not make wrong use of the name of the Lord your God; the Lord will not leave unpunished the man who misuses his name.

This Commandment is commonly ignored nowadays when so many people use the names of God and Christ as exclamations or swear words. St Paul condemns this.

St Paul's Letter to the Philippians, chapter 2, verses 5–11

Let your bearing towards one another arise out of your life in Christ Jesus. For the divine nature was his from the first; yet he did not think to snatch at equality with God, but made himself nothing, assuming the nature of a slave. Bearing the human likeness, revealed in human shape, he humbled himself, and in obedience accepted even death – death on a cross. Therefore God raised him to the heights and bestowed on him the name above all names, that at the name of Jesus every knee should bow – in heaven, on earth, and in the depths – and every tongue confess, 'Jesus Christ is Lord', to the glory of God the Father.

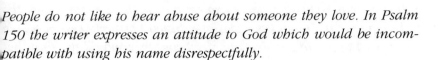

People do not like to hear abuse about someone they love. In Psalm 150 the writer expresses an attitude to God which would be incompatible with using his name disrespectfully.

Psalm 150

O Praise God in his holiness: praise
him in the firmament of his power.
Praise him in his noble acts: praise him
according to his excellent greatness.
Praise him in the sound of the trumpet:
praise him upon the lute and harp.
Praise him in the cymbals and dances:
praise him upon the strings and pipe.
Praise him upon the well-tuned cymbals:
praise him upon the loud cymbals.
Let every thing that hath breath:
praise the Lord.

Day 3

This is the fourth Commandment.

Book of Exodus, chapter 20, verses 8–11

Remember to keep the sabbath day holy. You have six days to labour and do all your work. But the seventh day is a sabbath of the Lord your God; that day you shall not do any work, you, your son or your daughter, your slave or your slave-girl, your cattle or the alien within your gates; for in six days the Lord made heaven and earth, the sea, and all that is in them, and on the seventh day he rested. Therefore the Lord blessed the sabbath day and declared it holy.

In the next reading, Jesus challenges the overstrict observance of the Sabbath by the Jewish leaders. Notice that Jesus does not reject the Commandment. He makes it positive. Instead of saying what people should not do on the Sabbath he says what they should do, and that is good to others. If Sunday were like any other day we should never have time to put our lives straight in this way.

St Luke's Gospel, chapter 13, verses 10–17

One Sabbath he was teaching in a synagogue, and there was a woman there possessed by a spirit that had crippled her for eighteen years. She was bent double and quite unable to stand up straight. When Jesus saw her he called her and said, 'You are rid of your trouble.' Then he laid his hands on her, and at once she straightened up and began to praise God. But the president of the synagogue, indignant with Jesus for healing on the Sabbath, intervened and said to the congregation, 'There are six working days: come and be cured on one of them, and not on the Sabbath.' The Lord gave him his answer: 'What hypocrites you are!' he said. 'Is there a single one of you who does not loose his ox or his donkey from the manger and take it out to water on the Sabbath? And here is this woman, a daughter of Abraham, who has been kept prisoner by Satan for eighteen long years: was it wrong for her to be freed from her bonds on the Sabbath?' At these words all his opponents were covered with confusion, while the mass of the people were delighted at all the wonderful things he was doing.

Day 4

This is the fifth Commandment.

Book of Exodus, chapter 20, verse 12

Honour your father and your mother, that you may live long in the land which the Lord your God is giving you.

*n the following reading, Jesus acts independently of his parents, but
nevertheless grows up in obedience to them.*

St Luke's Gospel, chapter 2, verses 41–52

Now it was the practice of his parents to go to Jerusalem every year
or the Passover festival; and when he was twelve, they made the pil-
rimage as usual. When the festive season was over and they started
or home, the boy Jesus stayed behind in Jerusalem. His parents did
not know of this; but thinking that he was with the party they jour-
neyed on for a whole day, and only then did they begin looking for
him among their friends and relations. As they could not find him they
returned to Jerusalem to look for him; and after three days they found
him sitting in the temple surrounded by the teachers, listening to them
and putting questions; and all who heard him were amazed at his
intelligence and the answers he gave. His parents were astonished to
see him there, and his mother said to him, 'My son, why have you
treated us like this? Your father and I have been searching for you in
great anxiety.' 'What made you search?' he said. 'Did you not know
that I was bound to be in my Father's house?' But they did not understand what he meant. Then he went back with them to Nazareth, and
continued to be under their authority; his mother treasured up all
these things in her heart. As Jesus grew up he advanced in wisdom
and in favour with God and men.

♦

This reading is from Smoke on the Mountain *by Joy Davidman.*

'Coping With Grandpa'

Once upon a time there was a little old man. His eyes blinked and
his hands trembled; when he ate he clattered the silverware dis-
tressingly, missed his mouth with the spoon as often as not, and
dribbled a bit of his food on the tablecloth. Now he lived with his
married son, having nowhere else to live, and his son's wife was a
modern young woman who knew that in-laws should not be toler-
ated in a woman's home. So she and her husband took the little old
man gently but firmly by the arm and led him to the corner of the
kitchen. There they set him on a stool and gave him his food, what
there was of it, in an earthenware bowl. From then on he always ate
in the corner, blinking at the table with wistful eyes.

One day his hands trembled rather more than usual, and the earthenware bowl fell and broke.

'If you are a pig,' said the daughter-in-law, 'you must eat out of a trough.' So they made him a little wooden trough, and he got his meals in that.

These people had a four-year-old son of whom they were very fond. One suppertime the young man noticed his boy playing intently with some bits of wood and asked what he was doing.

'I'm making a trough,' he said, smiling up for approval, 'to feed you and Mamma out of when I get big.'

The man and his wife looked at each other for a while and didn't say anything. Then they cried a little. Then they went to the corner and took the little old man by the arm and led him back to the table. They sat him in a comfortable chair and gave him his food on a plate, and from then on nobody ever scolded when he clattered or spilled or broke things.

One of Grimm's fairy tales, this anecdote has the crudity of the old simple days: the modern serpent's tooth method would be to lead Grandpa gently but firmly to the local asylum, there to tuck him out of sight as a case of senile dementia. But perhaps crudity is what we need to illustrate the naked and crude point of the Fifth Commandment: Honour your parents lest your children dishonour you. Or, in other words, a society that destroys the family destroys itself.

♦

One of the Commandments in the Book of Leviticus is respect for old people.

Book of Leviticus, chapter 19, verse 32

You shall rise in the presence of grey hairs, give honour to the aged and fear your God. I am the Lord.

Psalm 90, verses 10–11

...Seventy years is the span of our life,
eighty if our strength holds.

Teach us to order our days rightly
that we may enter the gate of wisdom.

♦

The following poem was found in the locker of an old lady who died in a nursing home.

'What Do You See?'

What do you see when you see me?
Are you thinking when you are looking at me
A crabbit old woman, not very wise,
Uncertain of habit, with far-away eyes,
Who unresisting or not lets you do as you will
With bathing and feeding the long day to fill?
Is that what you're thinking, is that what you see?
Then open your eyes, you're not looking at me.
I'll tell you who I am as I sit here so still,
As I do at your bidding, as I eat at your will.
I'm a small child of ten with a father and mother,
Brother and sister, who love one another;
A young girl of sixteen with wings on her feet,
Dreaming that now soon a lover she'll meet.
A bride soon at twenty – my heart gives a leap,
Remembering the vows that I promise to keep.
At twenty-five now I have young of my own
(Who need me to build a secure happy home):
A woman of thirty, my young now grow fast,
Bound to each other with ties that should last.
At forty, my young sons now grown and all gone,
But my man stays beside me to see I don't mourn.
At fifty once more babies play round my knee:
Again we know children, my loved one and me.
Dark days are upon me, my husband is dead:
I look at the future, I shudder with dread,
For my young are all busy rearing young of their own
And I think of the years and the love that I've known.
I'm an old woman now and Nature is cruel –
'Tis her jest to make old age look like a fool.
The body it crumbles, grace and vigour depart,
But inside this old carcass a young girl still dwells
And now and again my battered heart swells.

I remember the joys, I remember the pain,
And I'm loving and living all over again.
I think of the years all too few – gone too fast,
And accept the stark fact that nothing can last.
So open your eyes, open and see
Not a crabbit old woman: look closer – see me!

Day 5

This is the sixth Commandment.

Book of Exodus, chapter 20, verse 13

You shall not commit murder.

Christ comments on this Commandment.

St Matthew's Gospel, chapter 5, verses 21–26 and 38–48

'You have learned that our forefathers were told, "Do not commit murder; anyone who commits murder must be brought to judgement." But what I tell you is this: Anyone who nurses anger against his brother must be brought to judgement. If he abuses his brother he must answer for it to the court; if he sneers at him he will have to answer for it in the fires of hell.

'If, when you are bringing your gift to the altar, you suddenly remember that your brother has a grievance against you, leave your gift where it is before the altar. First go and make your peace with your brother, and only then come back and offer your gift.

'If someone sues you, come to terms with him promptly while you are both on your way to court; otherwise he may hand you over to the judge, and the judge to the constable, and you will be put in jail. I tell you, once you are there you will not be let out till you have paid the last farthing.'

'You have learned that they were told, "Eye for eye, tooth for tooth." But what I tell you is this: Do not set yourself against the man who wrongs you. If someone slaps you on the right cheek, turn and offer him your left. If a man wants to sue you for your shirt, let him have our coat as well. If a man in authority makes you go one mile, go with him two. Give when you are asked to give; and do not turn our back on a man who wants to borrow.

'You have learned that they were told, "Love your neighbour, hate our enemy." But what I tell you is this: Love your enemies and pray or your persecutors; only so can you be children of your heavenly ather, who makes his sun rise on good and bad alike, and sends the ain on the honest and the dishonest. If you love only those who ove you, what reward can you expect? Surely the tax-gatherers do s much as that. And if you greet only your brothers, what is there xtraordinary about that? Even the heathen do as much. There must e no limit to your goodness, as your heavenly Father's goodness nows no bounds.'

◆

his next passage shows that it is only when we regard others as less han human that we can see them as enemies.

'Prisoners'
by Yevgeny Yevtushenko

n '41 Mama took me back to Moscow. There I saw our enemies for he first time. If my memory is right, nearly twenty thousand German var prisoners were to be marched in a single column through the treets of Moscow.

The pavements swarmed with onlookers, cordoned off by sol-iers and police.

The crowd were mostly women – Russian women with hands oughened by hard work, lips untouched by lipstick and thin unched shoulders which had borne half the burden of the war. very one of them must have had a father or a husband, a brother or a son killed by the Germans.

They gazed with hatred in the direction from which the column vas to appear.

At last we saw it.

The generals marched at the head, massive chins stuck out, lips olded disdainfully, their whole demeanour meant to show superior-ty over their plebeian victors.

'They smell of eau-de-cologne, the bastards,' someone in the :rowd said with hatred.

The women were clenching their fists. The soldiers and police men had all they could do to hold them back.

All at once something happened to them.

They saw German soldiers, thin, unshaven, wearing dirty blood stained bandages, hobbling on crutches or leaning on the shoulder of their comrades; the soldiers walked with their heads down.

The street became dead silent – the only sound was the shuffling of boots and the thumping of crutches.

Then I saw an elderly woman in broken-down boots push herself forward and touch a policeman's shoulder, saying: 'Let me through. There must have been something about her that made him step aside

She went up to the column, took from inside her coat something wrapped in a coloured handkerchief and unfolded it. It was a crust of black bread. She pushed it awkwardly into the pocket of a soldier so exhausted that he was tottering on his feet. And now suddenly from every side women were running towards the soldiers, pushing into their hands bread, cigarettes, whatever they had.

The soldiers were no longer enemies.

They were people.

Day 6

This is the seventh Commandment.

Book of Exodus, chapter 20, verse 14

You shall not commit adultery.

Jesus comments on this Commandment.

St Matthew's Gospel, chapter 5, verses 27–28 and 31–32

'You have learned that they were told, "Do not commit adultery." But what I tell you is this: If a man looks on a woman with a lustful eye he has already committed adultery with her in his heart.

'They were told, "A man who divorces his wife must give her a note of dismissal." But what I tell you is this: If a man divorces his wife for any cause other than unchastity he involves her in adultery and anyone who marries a divorced woman commits adultery.'

◆

In this next story, the authorities are testing Jesus. The Jewish law stated that a woman convicted of adultery should be stoned to death. If Jesus had said that this should be carried out, where would be his credentials as a merciful man? If, however, he said she should be forgiven then they could accuse him of being soft on crime. Jesus does not condone the sin but he gives the woman another chance.

The story shows how careful we should be about judging other people.

St John's Gospel, chapter 8, verses 1–11

Jesus went unto the mount of Olives.

And early in the morning he came again into the Temple, and all the people came unto him; and he sat down, and taught them.

And the scribes and Pharisees brought unto him a woman taken in adultery; and when they had set her in the midst,

They say unto him, Master, this woman was taken in adultery, in the very act. Now Moses in the law commanded us, that such should be stoned: but what sayest thou?

This they said, tempting him, that they might have to accuse him. But Jesus stooped down, and with his finger wrote on the ground, as though he heard them not.

So when they continued asking him, he lifted up himself, and said unto them, He that is without sin among you, let him first cast a stone at her.

And again he stooped down, and wrote on the ground.

And they which heard it, being convicted by their own conscience, went out one by one, beginning at the eldest even unto the last: and Jesus was left alone, and the woman standing in the midst.

When Jesus had lifted up himself, and saw none but the woman, he said unto her, Woman, where are those thine accusers? Hath no man condemned thee?

She said, No man, Lord. And Jesus said unto her, Neither do I condemn thee: go, and sin no more.

Day 7

This is the eighth Commandment.

Book of Exodus, chapter 20, verse 15

You shall not steal.

The following readings explain fully the Jewish law on this subject.

Book of Leviticus, chapter 6, verses 1–5

The Lord spoke to Moses and said: When any person sins and commits a grievous fault against the Lord, whether he lies to a fellow-countryman about a deposit or contract, or a theft, or wrongs him by extortion, or finds lost property and then lies about it, and swears a false oath in regard to any sin of this sort that he commits – if he does this, thereby incurring guilt, he shall restore what he has stolen or gained by extortion, or the deposit left with him or the lost property which he found, or anything at all concerning which he swore a false oath. He shall make full restitution, adding one fifth to it, and give it back to the aggrieved party on the day when he offers his guilt-offering.

◆

St Paul's Letter to the Ephesians, chapter 4, verse 28

The thief must give up stealing, and instead work hard and honestly with his own hands, so that he may have something to share with the needy.

◆

In this next story, two attitudes to stealing are described. How might it be possible to change the attitude of the boy who steals? The other boy does not join in but he does not know how to react.

'Apostate'
by Forrest Reid

The stranger did not trouble to turn his head.

'What's your name?' I asked him uncomfortably.

I was sure he was going to tell me to mind my own business; but he didn't; he rose from his seat. 'Alan Cunningham,' he said. 'We'd better go and get some lemonade. There's a place just across the street.'

I had just taken my first sip when Alan leaned forward, and pointing to a shelf directly behind Mr Brown's head, asked, 'What are those?'

Mr Brown turned mechanically, and at the same instant Alan lifted a large flat package of chocolate from the counter and slipped it beneath his jacket.

'Which do you mean?' asked Mr Brown vaguely.

'Those green sweets. But it doesn't matter; I don't want any.'

There was not a glimmer of expression in his face or in his voice as he spoke. I was profoundly shocked, and what helped to trouble me was the fact that this boy had done what he had done so openly, without knowing whether I should object or not, without really knowing anything about me, and apparently without caring either.

We finished our lemonade (in my case with no great enjoyment) and came out into the sunlit street. He continued to walk beside me. Not a word about what had taken place passed between us, though the embarrassment and constraint appeared to be wholly mine.

'Shall I come round this afternoon?' he asked. 'Will you be here if I do?'

I hesitated, but he did not seem to be conscious that my reply was rather long in coming. He even put his hand on my shoulder as we walked slowly on up Mount Charles. Then I said 'Yes' but I did not look at him as I said it.

It was just before we reached the house that he took the package of chocolate from inside his jacket, and breaking it in half, handed one half to me. I shook my head and rang the bell.

'I'll chuck it away if you don't.'

'You can do as you like,' I answered. 'I don't want it.'

He stood for a moment in silence. 'Well, I'll leave it on the window sill. Somebody will see it and take it.'

Just then my eldest sister opened the door. He smiled at her and without the least hesitation, offered her the chocolate.

Day 8

The ninth Commandment is about telling lies.

Book of Exodus, chapter 20, verse 16

You shall not give false evidence against your neighbour.

There is a saying: 'Sticks and stones may break my bones but words, they cannot hurt me.' Many of us know that this is not true. For thousands of years, people have realized that talking behind the backs of others can be very destructive. The next reading is about rumour and gossip.

Book of Ecclesiasticus, chapter 28, verses 13–21 and 24–26

'Curses on the gossip and tale-bearer!
For they have been the ruin of many peaceable men.
The talk of a third party has wrecked the lives of many
and driven them from country to country;
it has destroyed fortified towns
and demolished the houses of the great.
The talk of a third party has brought divorce on staunch wives
and deprived them of all they have laboured for.
Whoever pays heed to it will never again find rest
or live in peace of mind.
The lash of a whip raises weals,
but the lash of a tongue breaks bones.
Many have been killed by the sword,
but not so many as by the tongue.
Happy the man who is sheltered from its onslaught,
who has not been exposed to its fury,
who has not borne its yoke,
or been chained with its fetters!
For its yoke is of iron,
its fetters of bronze.
The death it brings is an evil death;
better the grave than the tongue!...'

'As you enclose your garden with a thorn hedge,
and lock up your silver and gold,
so weigh your words and measure them,
and make a door and a bolt for your mouth.
Beware of being tripped by your tongue
and falling into the power of a lurking enemy.'

♦

Truth and honesty have been valued throughout the centuries, and written about by great thinkers of many nations.

The twentieth-century French writer and Christian philosopher Simone Weil wrote:

Christ likes us to prefer truth to him because, before being Christ, he is truth. If one turns aside from him to go towards the truth, one will not go far before falling into his arms.

The French author and poet Charles Péguy, who lived in the late nineteenth and early twentieth centuries, wrote:

He who does not bellow the truth when he knows the truth makes himself the accomplice of liars and forgers.

St Thomas Aquinas the medieval Christian philosopher wrote:

Truth is a divine thing, a friend more excellent than any human friend.

Guiseppe Prezzolini, an Italian, wrote in this century:

The essence of man lies in this, in his marvellous faculty for seeking truth, seeing it, loving it, and sacrificing himself to it.

Finally, Plato wrote in Greece in the fourth century before Christ:

Now I, Callicles, am persuaded of the truth of these things, and I consider how I shall present my soul whole and undefiled before the judge in that day. Renouncing the honours at which the world aims, I desire only to know the truth, and to live as well as I can, and, when I die, to die as well as I can. And, to the utmost of my power, I exhort all other men to do the same. And, in return for your exhortation of me, I exhort you also to take part in the great combat, which is the combat of life, and greater than every other earthly conflict.

Day 9

The tenth Commandment is about wanting things that belong to other people.

Book of Exodus, chapter 20, verse 17

You shall not covet your neighbour's house; you shall not covet your neighbour's wife, his slave, his slave-girl, his ox, his ass, or anything that belongs to him.

This next story is about greed and about relying on material things.

St Luke's Gospel, chapter 12, verses 13–21

A man in the crowd said to him, 'Master, tell my brother to divide the family property with me.' He replied, 'My good man, who set me over you to judge or arbitrate?' Then he said to the people, 'Beware! Be on your guard against greed of every kind, for even when a man has more than enough, his wealth does not give him life.' And he told them this parable: 'There was a rich man whose land yielded heavy crops. He debated with himself: "What am I to do? I have not the space to store my produce. This is what I will do," said he: "I will pull down my storehouses and build them bigger. I will collect in them all my corn and other goods, and then say to myself, 'Man, you have plenty of good things laid by, enough for many years: take life easy, eat, drink, and enjoy yourself.'" But God said to him, "You fool, this very night you must surrender your life; you have made your money – who will get it now?" That is how it is with the man who amasses wealth for himself and remains a pauper in the sight of God.'

◆

By contrast, here is a story told by Mother Teresa about the generosity of the poor.

A Gift for God

by Mother Teresa

Some weeks back I heard there was a Hindu family who had not eaten for some days – so I took some rice and I went to them. Before I knew where I was, the mother had divided the rice into two and she took the other half to the next-door neighbours, who happened to be a Muslim family. Then I asked her: 'How much will all of you have to share? There are ten of you with that bit of rice.' The mother replied, 'They have not eaten either.'

◆

Jesus also commented on the generosity of the poor in the following story.

St Mark's Gospel, chapter 12, verses 41–44

Once he was standing opposite the temple treasury, watching as people dropped their money into the chest. Many rich people were giving large sums. Presently there came a poor widow who dropped in two tiny coins, together worth a farthing. He called his disciples to him. 'I tell you this,' he said: 'this poor widow has given more than any of the others; for those others who have given had more than enough, but she, with less than enough, has given all that she had to live on.'

———◆———

Day 10

Jesus summarized the Ten Commandments in this passage.

St Mark's Gospel, chapter 12, verses 28–31

Then one of the lawyers, who had been listening to these discussions and had noted how well he answered, came forward and asked him, 'Which commandment is first of all?' Jesus answered, 'The first is, "Hear, O Israel: the Lord our God is the only Lord; love the Lord your God with all your heart, with all your soul, with all your mind and with all your strength." The second is this: "Love your neighbour as yourself." There is no other commandment greater than these.'

◆

The importance of our love for each other is expressed in the following passage.

From Resurrection
by Tolstoy

People think there are circumstances when one may deal with human beings without love, but no such circumstances ever exist. Inanimate objects may be dealt with without love: we may fell trees, bake bricks, hammer iron without love. But human beings cannot be handled without love, any more than bees can be handled without care. That is the nature of bees. If you handle bees carelessly you will harm the bees and yourself as well. And so it is with people. And it cannot be otherwise, because mutual love is the fundamental law of human life. It is true that a man cannot force himself to love in the way he can force himself to work, but it does not follow from this that men may be treated without love, especially if something is required from them. If you feel no love – leave people alone. Occupy yourself with things, with yourself, with anything you like, only not with men. Just as one can eat without harm and profitably only when one is hungry, so can one usefully and without injury deal with men only when one loves them. But once a man allows himself to treat men unlovingly, there are no limits to the cruelty and brutality he may inflict on others.

◆

Mother Teresa is famous for her care for the dying and destitute on the streets of Calcutta, but now there are groups of her Sisters of Charity all over the world. This is what she said after visiting England, about how we should show our love for each other:

A Gift for God

by Mother Teresa

You have a welfare state in England, but I have walked at night and gone into your homes and found people dying unloved. Here you have a different kind of poverty – a poverty of the spirit, of loneliness, and of being unwanted. And that is the worst disease in the world today; not tuberculosis or leprosy. I think England needs more and more for the people to know who the poor are. People in England should give their hearts to love the poor, and also their hands to serve them. And they cannot do that unless they know them, and knowledge will lead them to love, and love to service.

In England and other places, in Calcutta, in Melbourne, in New York, we find lonely people who are known by the number of their room. Why are we not there? Do we really know that there are some such people, maybe next-door to us? Maybe there is a blind man who would be happy if you would read the newspaper for him; maybe there is a rich person who has no one to visit him – he has plenty of other things, he is nearly drowned in them, but there is not that touch and he needs your touch. Some time back a very rich man came to our place, and he said to me: 'Please, either you or somebody, come to my house. I am nearly half-blind and my wife is nearly mental; our children have all gone abroad, and we are dying of loneliness, we are longing for the loving sound of a human voice.'

Let us not be satisfied with just giving money. Money is not enough, money can be got, but they need your hearts to love them. So, spread love everywhere you go: first of all in your own home. Give love to your children, to your wife or husband, to a next-door neighbour.

You ask how I should see the task of the Missionaries of Charity if I were a religious sister or priest in Surrey or Sussex. Well, the task of the Church in such places is much more difficult than what we face in Calcutta, Yemen, or anywhere else, where all the people need is dressing for their wounds, a bowl of rice and a 'cuddle', with someone telling them they are loved and wanted. In Surrey and Sussex the problems of your people are deep down, at the bottom of their hearts. They have to come to know you and trust you, to see you as a person with Christ's compassion and love, before their problems will emerge and you can help them. This takes a lot of time! Time for you to be people of prayer and time to give of yourself to each one of your people.

Day 11

Here are two more passages about loving our neighbour. The first is by an anonymous writer.

I shall pass through this world but once. Any good thing therefore that I can do, or any kindness that I can show to any human being, let me do it now. Let me not defer it or neglect it, for I shall not pass this way again.

♦

In the second passage, the writer assesses the demands of the Christian Gospel.

From Prayers of Life
by Michel Quoist

This evening, Lord, I am afraid.
I am afraid, for your Gospel is terrible.
It is easy to hear it preached,
It is relatively easy not to be shocked by it,
But it is very difficult to live it.

I am afraid of deluding myself, Lord.
I am afraid of being satisfied with my decent little life,
I am afraid of my good habits, for I take them for virtues;
I am afraid of my little efforts, for I take them for progress;
I am afraid of my activities; they make me think I am giving
myself.
I am afraid of my clever planning; I take it for success.
I am afraid of my influence, I imagine that it will transform lives;
I am afraid of what I give; it hides what I withhold;
I am afraid, Lord; there are people who are poorer than I;
Not so well-educated,
housed,
heated,
fed,
cared for,
loved.

I am afraid, Lord, for I do not do enough for them,
I do not do everything for them.
I should give everything,
I should give everything till there is not a single pain, a single
misery, a single sin in the world.
I should then give all, Lord, all the time.
I should give my life.

Lord, it is not true, is it?
It is not true for everyone,
I am exaggerating, I must be sensible!

Son, there is only *one* commandment,
For *everyone:*
You shall love with *all* your heart,
with *all* your soul,
with *all* your strength.

———◆———

Day 12

This is a passage from Jane Austen's Sense and Sensibility *and it shows how easy it is for one person to bring out the worst in another. Mr John Dashwood is a young man whose mother died; his father married again and had two daughters. In the course of time the father died, leaving his grand house, his wealth and his possessions to his son. So Mr John Dashwood is now a very rich young man, married to Fanny and they have a baby son, Harry.*

From Sense and Sensibility
by Jane Austen

Mrs John Dashwood did not at all approve of what her husband intended to do for his sisters. To take three thousand pounds from the fortune of their dear little boy, would be impoverishing him to the most dreadful degree. She begged him to think again on the subject. How could he answer it to himself to rob his child, and his only child too, of so large a sum? And what possible claim could the Miss Dashwoods, who were related to him only by half blood, which she considered as no relationship at all, have on his generosity to so large an amount. It was very well known that no affection was ever supposed to exist between the children of any man by different marriages; and why was he to ruin himself, and their poor little Harry, by giving away all his money to his half sisters?

'It was my father's last request to me', replied her husband, 'that I should assist his widow and daughters.'

'He did not know what he was talking of, I dare say; ten to one but he was light-headed at the time. Had he been in his right senses, he could not have thought of such a thing as begging you to give away half your fortune from your own child.'

'He did not stipulate for any particular sum, my dear Fanny; he only requested me, in general terms, to assist them, and make their situation more comfortable than it was in his power to do. Perhaps it would have been as well if he had left it wholly to myself. He could hardly suppose I should neglect them. But as he required the promise, I could not do less than give it: at least I thought so at the time. The promise, therefore, was given, and must be performed. Something must be done for them whenever they leave Norland and settle in a new home.'

'Well, then, *let* something be done for them; but *that* something need not be three thousand pounds. Consider,' she added, 'that when the money is once parted with, it never can return. Your sisters will marry, and it will be gone for ever. If, indeed, it could ever be restored to our poor little boy.'

'Why, to be sure,' said her husband, very gravely, 'that would make a great difference. The time may come when Harry will regret that so large a sum was parted with. If he should have a numerous family, for instance, it would be a very convenient addition.'

'To be sure it would.'

'Perhaps, then, it would be better for all parties if the sum were diminished one half. Five hundred pounds would be a prodigious increase to their fortunes!'

'Oh! beyond any thing great! What brother on earth would do half so much for his sisters, even if *really* his sisters! And as it is – only half blood! – But you have such a generous spirit!'

'I would not wish to do any thing mean,' he replied. 'One had rather, on such occasions, do too much than too little. No one, at least, can think I have not done enough for them: even themselves they can hardly expect more.'

'There is no knowing what *they* may expect,' said the lady, 'but we are not to think of their expectations: the question is, what you can afford to do.'

'Certainly – and I think I may afford to give them five hundred pounds a-piece. As it is, without any addition of mine, they will each have above a thousand pounds on their mother's death – a very comfortable fortune for any young woman.'

'To be sure it is: and, indeed, it strikes me that they can want no addition at all. They will have ten thousand pounds divided amongst them. If they marry, they will be sure of doing well, and if they do not, they may all live very comfortably together on the interest of ten thousand pounds.'

'That is very true, and, therefore, I do not know whether, upon the whole, it would not be more advisable to do something for their mother while she lives rather than for them – something of the annuity kind I mean. My sisters would feel the good effects of it as well as herself. A hundred a year would make them all perfectly comfortable.'

His wife hesitated a little, however, in giving her consent to this plan.

'To be sure,' said she, 'it is better than parting with fifteen hundred pounds at once. But then if Mrs Dashwood should live fifteen years we shall be completely taken in.'

'Fifteen years! my dear Fanny; her life cannot be worth half that purchase.'

'Certainly not; but if you observe, people always live for ever when there is any annuity to be paid them; and she is very stout and healthy, and hardly forty. An annuity is a very serious business; it comes over and over every year, and there is no getting rid of it. You are not aware of what you are doing. I have known a great deal of the trouble of annuities; for my mother was clogged with the payment of three to old superannuated servants by my father's will, and it is amazing how disagreeable she found it. Twice every year these annuities were to be paid; and then there was the trouble of getting it to them; and then one of them was said to have died, and afterwards it turned out to be no such thing. My mother was quite sick of it. Her income was not her own, she said, with such perpetual claims on it; and it was the more unkind in my father, because, otherwise, the money would have been entirely at my mother's disposal, without any restriction whatever. It has given me such an abhorrence of annuities, that I am sure I would not pin myself down to the payment of one for all the world.'

'It is certainly an unpleasant thing', replied Mr Dashwood, 'to have those kind of yearly drains on one's income. One's fortune, as your mother justly says, is *not* one's own. To be tied down to the regular payment of such a sum, on every rent day, is by no means desirable; it takes away one's independence.'

'Undoubtedly; and after all you have no thanks for it. They think themselves secure, you do no more than what is expected, and it raises no gratitude at all. If I were you, whatever I did should be done at my own discretion entirely. I would not bind myself to allow them any thing yearly. It may be very inconvenient some years to spare a hundred, or even fifty pounds from our own expenses.'

'I believe you are right, my love; it will be better that there should be no annuity in the case; whatever I may give them occasionally will be of far greater assistance than a yearly allowance, because they would only enlarge their style of living if they felt sure of a larger income, and would not be sixpence the richer for it at the end of the year. It will certainly be much the best way. A present of fifty pounds now and then, will prevent their ever being distressed for money, and will, I think, be amply discharging my promise to my father.'

'To be sure it will. Indeed, to say the truth, I am convinced within myself that your father had no idea of your giving them any money at all. The assistance he thought of, I dare say, was only such as might be reasonably expected of you; for instance, such as looking out for a comfortable small house for them, helping them to move their things, and sending them presents of fish and game, and so forth, whenever they are in season. I'll lay my life that he meant nothing farther; indeed, it would be very strange and unreasonable if he did. Do but consider, my dear Mr Dashwood, how excessively comfortable your mother-in-law and her daughters may live on the interest of seven thousand pounds, besides the thousand pounds belonging to each of the girls, which brings them in fifty pounds a-year a-piece, and, of course, they will pay their mother for their board out of it. Altogether, they will have five hundred a-year amongst them, and what on earth can four women want for more than that? They will live so cheap!

heir housekeeping will be nothing at all. They will have no carriage, o horses, and hardly any servants; they will keep no company, and an have no expenses of any kind! Only conceive how comfortable ley will be! Five hundred a-year! I am sure I cannot imagine how they ill spend half of it; and as to your giving them more, it is quite absurd think of it. They will be much more able to give *you* something.'

'Upon my word,' said Mr Dashwood, 'I believe you are perfectly ght. My father certainly could mean nothing more by his request to le than what you say. I clearly understand it now, and I will rictly fulfil my engagement by such acts of assistance and kindness them as you have described. When my mother removes into anoth- r house my services shall be readily given to accommodate her as far s I can. Some little present of furniture too may be acceptable then.'

'Certainly,' returned Mrs John Dashwood. 'But however, *one* thing lust be considered. When your father and mother moved to Norland, lough the furniture of Stanhill was sold, all the china, plate, and linen as saved, and is now left to your mother. Her house will therefore e almost completely fitted up as soon as she takes it.'

'That is a material consideration undoubtedly. A valuable legacy ldeed! And yet some of the plate would have been a very pleasant ddition to our own stock here.'

'Yes; and the set of breakfast china is twice as handsome as what elongs to this house. A great deal too handsome, in my opinion, for ny place *they* can ever afford to live in. But, however, so it is. Your ither thought only of *them*. And I must say this: that you owe no articular gratitude to him, nor attention to his wishes, for we very ell know that if he could, he would have left almost every thing in le world to *them*.'

This argument was irresistible. It gave to his intentions whatever f decision was wanting before; and he finally resolved, that it would e absolutely unnecessary, if not highly indecorous, to do more for le widow and children of his father, than such kind of neighbourly cts as his own wife pointed out.

10
Spiritual experiences

The passages about religious experiences in this section could be used from time to time rather than as a sequence. They vary in tone and content but the language is often heightened or poetic because the writer is attempting to describe the indescribable.

Day 1

The writer Victor Gollancz describes religious experience in these words:

There are moments in some people's lives when a veil seems suddenly drawn aside from the universe, and they see everything as divine. Such visions are always accompanied by a feeling of peculiar joy, and by a sense, very difficult to convey, of certainty, of inevitability, of everything being utterly 'right'.

◆

The first example of such a vision is the story of Jacob's ladder. Jacob experience is in a dream.

Book of Genesis, chapter 28, verses 10–17

Jacob set out from Beersheba and went on his way towards Harran. He came to a certain place and stopped there for the night, because the sun had set; and, taking one of the stones there, he made it a pillow for his head and lay down to sleep. He dreamt that he saw a ladder, which rested on the ground with its top reaching to heaven and angels of God were going up and down upon it. The Lord was standing beside him and said, 'I am the Lord, the God of your father Abraham and the God of Isaac. This land on which you are lying will give to you and your descendants. They shall be countless as the dust upon the earth, and you shall spread far and wide, to north and south, to east and west. All the families of the earth shall pray to be blessed as you and your descendants are blessed. I will be with you, and I will protect you wherever you go and will bring you back to this land; for I will not leave you until I have done all that I have promised.' Jacob woke from his sleep and said, 'Truly the Lord is in this place, and I did not know it.' Then he was afraid and said, 'How fearsome is this place! This is no other than the house of God, this is the gate of heaven.'

♦

In this poem, the poet explains how a feeling of God's presence can happen here and now in our own mundane world.

'The Kingdom of God'
by Francis Thompson

O World invisible, we view thee,
O World intangible, we touch thee,
O World unknowable, we know thee,
Inapprehensible, we clutch thee!

Does the fish soar to find the ocean,
The eagle plunge to find the air –
That we ask of the stars in motion
If they have rumour of thee there?

Not where the wheeling systems darken,
And our benumbed conceiving soars! –
The drift of pinions, would we hearken,
Beats at our own clay-shuttered doors.

The angels keep their ancient places; –
Turn but a stone, and start a wing!
'Tis ye, 'tis your estranged faces,
That miss the many-splendoured thing.

But (when so sad thou canst not sadder)
Cry; – and upon thy so sore loss
Shall shine the traffic of Jacob's ladder
Pitched betwixt Heaven and Charing Cross.

Yea, in the night, my Soul, my daughter,
Cry, – clinging Heaven by the hems;

And lo, Christ walking on the water,
Not of Gennesareth, but Thames!

Day 2

This vision of God was experienced by the prophet Elijah.

First Book of Kings, chapter 19, verses 9–13

And he came thither unto a cave, and lodged there; and, behold, the word of the Lord came to him, and he said unto him, What doest thou here, Elijah?

And he said, I have been very jealous for the Lord God of hosts: for the children of Israel have forsaken thy covenant, thrown down thine altars, and slain thy prophets with the sword; and I, even I only, am left; and they seek my life, to take it away.

And he said, Go forth, and stand upon the mount before the Lord. And, behold, the Lord passed by, and a great and strong wind rent the mountains, and brake in pieces the rocks before the Lord; but the Lord was not in the wind: and after the wind an earthquake; but the Lord was not in the earthquake:

And after the earthquake a fire; but the Lord was not in the fire: and after the fire a still small voice.

And it was so, when Elijah heard it, that he wrapped his face in his mantle, and went out, and stood in the entering in of the cave.

♦

St Teresa of Ávila wrote:

It is worth remembering what St Augustine says. He looked everywhere for God, and at last came to find him in himself. It is important, especially for someone who is worried, to realize this truth, and to know that he or she need not go to heaven to speak with God the father, or to enjoy his presence. And there is no need for anyone to speak out loud – for however quietly we may speak, God is so near that he will hear us. There is no need either to take flight to look for God, because we can always settle ourselves in peace and quiet, and see God there, within ourselves.

◆

A similar idea is expressed in this poem.

'The Voice of God'
by Stephen Crane

The livid lightnings flashed in the clouds:
The leaden thunders crashed.
A worshipper raised his arm.
'Hearken! hearken! The voice of God!'
'Not so,' said a man.
'The voice of God whispers in the heart
So softly
That the soul pauses,
Making no noise,
And strives for these melodies,
Distant, sighing, like faintest breath,
And all the being is still to hear.'

———◆———

Day 3

In the next passage, the poet Wordsworth is inspired by the 'beauteous forms' in the natural world. In their presence or even just remembering them, he feels at one with a great spirit, and this has a profound influence on his life.

From 'Lines composed a few miles above Tintern Abbey'
by William Wordsworth

These beauteous forms,
Through a long absence, have not been to me
As is a landscape to a blind man's eye:
But oft, in lonely rooms, and 'mid the din
Of towns and cities, I have owed to them,
In hours of weariness, sensations sweet,
Felt in the blood, and felt along the heart;
And passing even into my purer mind,
With tranquil restoration: – feelings too
Of unremembered pleasure: such, perhaps,

As have no slight or trivial influence
On that best portion of a good man's life,
His little, nameless, unremembered, acts
Of kindness and of love. Nor less, I trust,
To them I may have owed another gift,
Of aspect more sublime; that blessed mood,
In which the burthen of the mystery,
In which the heavy and the weary weight
Of all this unintelligible world,
Is lightened: – that serene and blessed mood,
In which the affections gently lead us on, –
Until, the breath of this corporeal frame
And even the motion of our human blood
Almost suspended, we are laid asleep
In body, and become a living soul:
While with an eye made quiet by the power
Of harmony, and the deep power of joy,
We see into the life of things.
For I have learned
To look on nature, not as in the hour
Of thoughtless youth; but hearing oftentimes
The still, sad music of humanity,
Nor harsh not grating, though of ample power
To chasten and subdue. And I have felt
A presence that disturbs me with the joy
Of elevated thoughts; a sense sublime
Of something far more deeply interfused,
Whose dwelling is the light of setting suns,
And the round ocean and the living air,
And the blue sky, and in the mind of man:
A motion and a spirit, that impels
All thinking things, all objects of all thought,
And rolls through all things. Therefore am I still
A lover of the meadows and the woods,
And mountains; and of all that we behold
From this green earth; of all the mighty world
Of eye, and ear, – both what they half create,
And what perceive; well pleased to recognize
In nature and the language of the sense

The anchor of my purest thoughts, the nurse,
The guide, the guardian of my heart, and soul
Of all my moral being.

Day 4

This was the 'Vision of God' seen by St John.

Book of Revelation, chapter 4, verses 1–11

After this I looked, and there before my eyes was a door opened in heaven; and the voice that I had first heard speaking to me like a trumpet said, 'Come up here, and I will show you what must happen hereafter.' At once I was caught up by the Spirit. There in heaven stood a throne, and on the throne sat one whose appearance was like the gleam of jasper and cornelian; and round the throne was a rainbow, bright as an emerald. In a circle about this throne were twenty-four other thrones, and on them sat twenty-four elders, robed in white and wearing crowns of gold. From the throne went out flashes of lightning and peals of thunder. Burning before the throne were seven flaming torches, the seven spirits of God and in front of it stretched what seemed a sea of glass, like a sheet of ice.

In the centre, round the throne itself, were four living creatures, covered with eyes, in front and behind. The first creature was like a lion, the second like an ox, the third had a human face, the fourth was like an eagle in flight. The four living creatures, each of them with six wings, had eyes all over, inside and out; and by day and by night without a pause they sang:

'Holy, holy, holy is God the sovereign Lord of all, who was, and is, and is to come!'

As often as the living creatures give glory and honour and thanks to the One who sits on the throne, who lives for ever and ever, the twenty-four elders fall down before the One who sits on the throne and worship him who lives for ever and ever; and as they lay their crowns before the throne they cry:

'Thou art worthy, O Lord our God, to receive glory and honour and power, because thou didst create all things; by thy will they were created, and have their being!'

◆

By contrast, in this passage the writer takes the view of a man whose vision is not clear. He knows there is something wrong with his life and that he needs to change direction but he does not know the way. The Evangelist of the story has to point this out to him.

From The Pilgrim's Progress
by John Bunyan

Then said Evangelist, If this be thy condition, why standest thou still? He answered, Because I know not whither to go. Then he gave him a parchment roll; and there was written within, 'Flee from the wrath to come!' The man, therefore, read it; and looking upon Evangelist very carefully, said, Whither must I fly? Then said Evangelist, pointing with his finger over a very wide field, Do you see yonder Wicket-gate? The man said, No. Then said the other, Do you see yonder shining light? He said, I think I do. Then said Evangelist, Keep that light in your eye, and go up directly thereto, so shalt thou see the gate; at which, when thou knockest, it shall be told thee what thou shalt do. So I saw in my dream that the man began to run.

◆

Day 5

Here are two different religious experiences. The first is by the Russian writer Turgenev, and it takes place in the presence of other people.

I saw myself, in dream, a youth, almost a boy, in a low-pitched wooden church. The slim wax candles gleamed, spots of red, before the old pictures of the saints.

A ring of coloured light encircled each tiny flame. Dark and dim it was in the church... But there stood before me many people. All fair-haired, peasant heads. From time to time they began swaying, falling, rising again, like the ripe ears of wheat, when the wind of summer passes in slow undulation over them.

All at once some man came up from behind and stood beside me. I did not turn towards him; but at once I felt that this man was Christ.

Emotion, curiosity, awe overmastered me suddenly. I made an effort ... and looked at my neighbour.

A face like everyone's, a face like all men's faces. The eyes looked a little upwards, quietly and intently. The lips closed, but not compressed; the upper lip, as it were, resting on the lower; a small beard parted in two. The hands folded and still. And the clothes on him like everyone's.

'What sort of Christ is this?' I thought. 'Such an ordinary, ordinary man! It can't be!'

I turned away. But I had hardly turned my eyes away from this ordinary man when I felt again that it really was none other than Christ standing beside me.

Again I made an effort over myself... And again the same face, like all men's faces, the same everyday though unknown features.

And suddenly my heart sank, and I came to myself. Only then I realized that just such a face – a face like all men's faces – is the face of Christ.

♦

The second experience is from a postcard sent by the American poet Sylvia Plath to her mother on 7th January 1956. Writing from Nice in France, she tells of the afternoon she took a motor scooter inland to Vence, where there is a beautiful chapel decorated by the painter Matisse.

How can I describe the beauty of the country? Everything is so small, close, exquisite and fertile. Terraced gardens on steep slopes of rich, red earth, orange and lemon trees, olive orchards, tiny pink and peach houses. To Vence – small, on a sun-warmed hill, uncommercial, slow, peaceful. Walked to Matisse chapel – small, pure, clean-cut. White, with blue-tile roof sparkling in the sun. But shut! Only open to public two days a week. A kindly talkative peasant told me stories of how rich people came daily in large cars from Italy, Germany, Sweden, etc., and were not admitted, even for large sums of money. I was desolate and wandered to the back of the walled nunnery, where I could see a corner of the chapel and sketched it, feeling like Alice outside the garden, watching the white doves and orange trees. Then I went back to the front and stared with my face through the barred gate. I began to cry. I knew it was so lovely inside, pure white with the sun through blue, yellow and green stained windows: Then I heard a voice. 'Ne pleurez plus, entrez,' (do not cry any more, come in) and the Mother Superior let me in, after denying all the wealthy people in cars.

I just knelt in the heart of the sun and the colours of the sky, sea and sun, in the pure white heart of the chapel. 'Vous êtes si gentille,' (you are so kind) I stammered. The nun smiled. 'C'est la miséricorde de Dieu.' (it is the mercy of God). It was.

Day 6

In this passage, Ratty and Mole are rowing along the river at dawn, looking for a lost baby otter.

From The Wind In The Willows
by Kenneth Grahame.

Breathless and transfixed the Mole stopped rowing as the liquid run of that glad piping broke on him like a wave, caught him up, and possessed him utterly. He saw the tears on his comrade's cheeks, and bowed his head and understood. For a space they hung there, brushed by the purple loosestrife that fringed the bank; then the clear imperious summons that marched hand-in-hand with the intoxicating melody imposed its will on Mole, and mechanically he bent to his oars again. And the light grew steadily stronger, but no birds sang as they were wont to do at the approach of dawn; and but for the heavenly music all was marvellously still.

On either side of them, as they glided onwards, the rich meadowgrass seemed that morning of a freshness and a greenness unsurpassable. Never had they noticed the roses so vivid, the willowherb so riotous, the meadow-sweet so odorous and pervading. Then the murmur of the approaching weir began to hold the air, and they felt a consciousness that they were nearing the end, whatever it might be, that surely awaited their expedition.

A wide half-circle of foam and glinting lights and shining shoulders of green water, the great weir closed the backwater from bank to bank, troubled all the quiet surface with twirling eddies and floating foam-streaks, and deadened all other sounds with its solemn and soothing rumble. In midmost of the stream, embraced in the weir's shimmering arm-spread, a small island lay anchored, fringed close with willow and silver birch and alder. Reserved, shy, but full of significance, it hid whatever it might hold behind a veil, keeping it till the hour should come, and, with the hour, those who were called and chosen.

Slowly, but with no doubt or hesitation whatever, and in something of a solemn expectancy, the two animals passed through the broken, tumultuous water and moored their boat at the flowery margin of the island. In silence they landed, and pushed through the blossom and scented herbage and undergrowth that led up to the level ground, till they stood on a little lawn of a marvellous green, set round with Nature's own orchard-trees – crab-apple, wild cherry, and sloe.

'This is the place of my song-dream, the place the music played to me,' whispered the Rat, as if in a trance. 'Here, in this holy place, here if anywhere, surely we shall find Him!'

Then suddenly the Mole felt a great Awe fall upon him, an awe that turned his muscles to water, bowed his head, and rooted his feet to the ground. It was no panic terror – indeed he felt wonderfully at peace and happy – but it was an awe that smote and held him and, without seeing, he knew it could only mean that some august Presence was very, very near. With difficulty he turned to look for his friend, and saw him at his side cowed, stricken, and trembling violently. And still there was utter silence in the populous bird-haunted branches around them; and still the light grew and grew.

Perhaps he would never have dared to raise his eyes, but that, though the piping was now hushed, the call and the summons seemed still dominant and imperious. He might not refuse, were Death himself waiting to strike him instantly, once he had looked with mortal eye on things rightly kept hidden. Trembling he obeyed, and raised his humble head; and then, in that utter clearness of the imminent dawn, while Nature, flushed with fullness of incredible colour, seemed to hold her breath for the event, he looked in the very eyes of the Friend and Helper; saw the backward sweep of the curved horns, gleaming in the growing daylight; saw the stern, hooked nose between the kindly eyes that were looking down on them humorously, while the bearded mouth broke into a half-smile at the corners; saw the rippling muscles on the arms that lay across the broad chest, the long supple hand still holding the pan-pipes only just fallen away from the parted lips; saw the splendid curves of the shaggy limbs disposed in majestic ease on the sward; saw, last of all, nestling between his very hooves, sleeping soundly in entire peace and contentment, the little, round, podgy, childish form of the baby otter. All this he saw, for one moment breathless and intense, vivid on the morning sky; and still, as he looked, he lived; and still, as he lived, he wondered.

'Rat!' he found breath to whisper, shaking. 'Are you afraid?'

'Afraid?' murmured the Rat, his eyes shining with unutterable love. 'Afraid! Of *Him*? O, never, never! And yet – and yet – O, Mole, I am afraid!'

Then the two animals, crouching to the earth, bowed their heads and did worship.

Sudden and magnificent, the sun's broad golden disc showed itself over the horizon facing them; and the first rays, shooting across the level water-meadows, took the animals full in the eyes and dazzled them. When they were able to look once more, the Vision had vanished, and the air was full of the carol of birds that hailed the dawn.

As they stared blankly, in dumb misery deepening as they slowly realized all they had seen and all they had lost, a capricious little breeze, dancing up from the surface of the water, tossed the aspens, shook the dewy roses, and blew lightly and caressingly in their faces, and with its soft touch came instant oblivion. For this is the last best gift that the kindly demigod is careful to bestow on those to whom he has revealed himself in their helping: the gift of forgetfulness. Lest the awful remembrance should remain and grow, and overshadow mirth and pleasure, and the great haunting memory should spoil all the afterlives of little animals helped out of difficulties, in order that they should be happy and lighthearted as before.

Day 7

This is the final passage from the novel Kim. *It is the story of a young boy who becomes attached to a Tibetan Buddhist monk, Teshoo Lama. The monk tells Kim about his experience of death when he felt united to the Great Soul. He returns from the great happiness of this because Kim still needs his guidance in this world. Although written by a Christian author, this describes a Buddhist spiritual experience.*

From Kim
by Rudyard Kipling

When we came out of the Hills, I was troubled for thee and for other matters which I held in my heart. The boat of my soul lacked direction; I could not see into the Cause of Things. So I gave thee over to the virtuous woman altogether. I took no food. I drank no water. Still I saw not the Way. They pressed food upon me and cried at my shut door. So I removed myself to a hollow under a tree. I took no food. I took no water. I sat in meditation two days and two nights, abstracting my mind; inbreathing and outbreathing in the required manner...

Upon the second night – so great was my reward – the wise Soul loosed itself from the silly Body and went free. This I have never before attained, though I have stood on the threshold of it. Consider, for it is a marvel! 'A marvel indeed. Two days and two nights without food. Where was the Sahiba?' said Kim under his breath.

'Yea, my Soul went free, and, wheeling like an eagle, saw indeed that there was no Teshoo Lama nor any other soul. As a drop draws to water, so my Soul drew near to the Great Soul which is beyond all things. At that point, exalted in contemplation, I saw all Hind, from Ceylon in the sea to the Hills, and my own Painted Rocks at Such-zen; I saw every camp and village, to the least, where we have ever rested. I saw them at one time and in one place, for they were within the Soul. By this I knew the Soul had passed beyond the illusion of Time and Space and of Things. By this I knew that I was free. I saw thee lying in thy cot, and I saw thee falling downhill under the idolater – at one time, in one place, in my Soul, which, as I say, had touched the Great Soul. Also I saw the stupid body of Teshoo Lama lying down, and the hakim from Dacca kneeled beside, shouting in its ear. Then my Soul was alone, and I saw nothing, for I was all things, having reached the Great Soul. And I meditated a thousand thousand years, passionless, well aware of the Causes of all Things. Then a voice cried: 'What shall come to the boy if thou art dead?' and I was shaken back and forth in myself with pity for thee; and I said: 'I will return to my chela, lest he miss the Way.' Upon this my Soul, which is the Soul of Teshoo Lama, withdrew itself from the Great Soul with strivings and yearnings and retchings and agonies not to be told. As the egg from the fish, as the fish from the water, as the water from the cloud, as the cloud from the thick air, so put forth, so leaped out, so drew away, so fumed up the Soul of Teshoo Lama from the Great Soul. Then a voice cried: 'The River! Take heed to the River!' and I looked down upon all the world, which was as I had seen it before – one in time, one in place – and I saw plainly the River of the Arrow at my feet. At that hour my Soul was hampered by some evil or another whereof I was not wholly cleansed, and it lay upon my arms and coiled round my waist; but I put it aside, and I cast forth as an eagle in my fight for the very place of the River. I pushed aside world upon world for thy sake. I saw the River below me – the River of the Arrow – and, descending, the waters of it closed over me; and behold I was again in the body of Teshoo Lama, but free from sin, and the hakim from Dacca bore up my head in the waters of the River. It is here! It is behind the mango-tope here – even here!'

'Allah kerim! Oh, well that the Babu was by! Wast thou very wet?'

'Why should I regard? I remember the hakim was concerned for the body of Teshoo Lama. He haled it out of the holy water in his hands, and there came afterwards thy horse-seller from the North with a cot and men, and they put the body on the cot and bore it up to the Sahiba's house.'

'What said the Sahiba?'

'I was meditating in that body, and did not hear. So thus the Search is ended. For the merit that I have acquired, the River of the Arrow is here. It broke forth at our feet, as I have said. I have found it. Son of my Soul, I have wrenched my Soul back from the Threshold of Freedom to free thee from all sin – as I am free, and sinless! Just is the Wheel! Certain is our deliverance! Come!'

He crossed his hands on his lap and smiled, as a man may who has won salvation for himself and his beloved.

11
Praise and thanksgiving

Gathered loosely under this definition, the passages in this section are useful for special occasions: for the beginning and ending of terms; for harvest festivals; or for any celebrations or commemorations.

Day 1

These words are from a famous poetic passage in which the writer looks at the pattern of human life which we can perceive, and at the mystery beyond it which we may feel but cannot define.

Book of Ecclesiastes, chapter 3, verses 1–15

For everything there is a season,
and a time for every matter under heaven:
a time to be born, and a time to die;
a time to plant, and a time to pluck up what is planted;
a time to kill, and a time to heal;
a time to break down, and a time to build up;
a time to weep, and a time to laugh;
a time to mourn, and a time to dance;
a time to cast away stones, and a time to gather stones together;
a time to embrace, and a time to refrain from embracing;
a time to seek, and a time to lose;
a time to keep, and a time to cast away;
a time to rend, and a time to sew;
a time to keep silence, and a time to speak;
a time to love, and a time to hate;
a time for war, and a time for peace.

What gain has the worker from his toil? I have seen the business that God has given to the sons of men to be busy with. He hath made every thing beautiful in its time: also he has put eternity into man's mind, yet so that he cannot find out what God has done from the beginning to the end.

I know that there is nothing better for them, than to be happy and enjoy themselves as long as they live. And that it is God's gift to man that everyone should eat and drink and take pleasure in all his toil. I know that, whatever God does endures for ever: nothing can be added to it, nor anything taken from it: God has made it so, in order that men should fear before him. That which is already has been; that which is to be, already has been: and God sees what has been driven away.

Day 2

This passage (often used for commemoration services) sings the praises of great people of the past, both the famous and the unknown, who have shaped our world.

Book of Ecclesiasticus, chapter 44, verses 1–15

Let us now praise famous men, and our fathers in their generations. The Lord apportioned to them great glory, his majesty from the beginning. There were those who ruled in their kingdoms, and were men renowned for their power, giving counsel by their understanding, and proclaiming prophecies; leaders of the people in their deliberations and in understanding of learning for the people, wise in their words of instruction; those who composed musical tunes, and set forth verses in writing; rich men furnished with resources, living peaceably in their habitations – all these were honoured in their generations, and were the glory of their times.

There are some of them who have left a name, so that men declare their praise. And there are some who have no memorial, who have perished as though they had not lived; they have become as though they had not been born, and so have their children after them.

But these were men of mercy, whose righteous deeds have not been forgotten; their prosperity will remain with their descendants, and their inheritance to their children's children. Their descendants stand by the covenants; their children also, for their sake. Their

osterity will continue for ever, and their glory will not be blotted
ut. Their bodies were buried in peace, and their name lives to all
enerations. Peoples will declare their wisdom, and the congrega-
ion proclaims their praise.

Day 3

hese passages are about wisdom, its nature and its value.
    T S Eliot wrote:

Where is the wisdom we have lost in knowledge?
Where is the knowledge we have lost in information?

♦

*liot points out that those who are well informed or knowledgeable
ire not necessarily wise. The nature of political wisdom is clear in this
>assage from the First Book of Kings. Solomon, who became king of
srael after the death of his father, King David, had a dream in which
God asked him what he wanted as a gift. This was his reply.*

First Book of Kings, chapter 3, verses 7–15

Now, O Lord my God, thou hast made thy servant king in place of
ny father David, though I am a mere child, unskilled in leadership.
And I am here in the midst of thy people, the people of thy choice,
oo many to be numbered or counted. Give thy servant, therefore, a
1eart with skill to listen, so that he may govern thy people justly and
listinguish good from evil. For who is equal to the task of govern-
ng this great people of thine?' The Lord was well pleased that
iolomon had asked for this, and he said to him, 'Because you have
isked for this, and not for long life for yourself, or for wealth, or for
he lives of your enemies, but have asked for discernment in admin-
stering justice, I grant your request; I give you a heart so wise and
o understanding that there has been none like you before your time
1or will be after you. I give you furthermore those things for which
ou did not ask, such wealth and honour as no king of your time
:an match. And if you conform to my ways and observe my ordi-
1ances and commandments, as your father David did, I will give you
ong life.' Then he awoke, and knew it was a dream.

◆

In this next passage it is the spiritual nature of wisdom which is apparent. God is the source of wisdom.

Book of Ecclesiasticus, chapter I, verses 1–10 and 19

All wisdom cometh from the Lord, and is with him for ever. Who can number the sand of the sea, and the drops of rain, and the days of eternity? Who can find out the height of heaven, and the breadth of the earth, and the deep, and wisdom? Wisdom hath been created before all things, and the understanding of prudence from everlasting. The word of God most high is the fountain of wisdom; and her ways are everlasting commandments.

To whom hath the root of wisdom been revealed? Or who hath known her wise counsels?

There is one wise and greatly to be feared, the Lord sitting upon his throne. He created her, and saw her, and numbered her, and poured her out upon all his works. She is with all flesh according to his gift, and he hath given her to them that love him.

Wisdom raineth down skill and knowledge of understanding, and exalteth them to honour that hold her fast.

◆

The next reading is about the great value of wisdom.

Book of Proverbs, chapter 3, verses 13–18

Happy is the man that findeth wisdom, and the man that getteth understanding.

For the merchandise of it is better than the merchandise of silver, and the gain thereof than fine gold.

She is more precious than rubies: and all the things thou canst desire are not to be compared unto her.

Length of days is in her right hand: and in her left hand riches and honour.

Her ways are ways of pleasantness, and all her paths are peace.

She is a tree of life to them that lay hold upon her: and happy is every one that retaineth her.

Day 4

These passages are about seeing God in his creation. They can be used for celebrations such as Harvest Festivals.

Psalm 104, verses 2–5, 13–15 and 24–33

Praise the Lord, O my soul: O Lord
my God thou art become exceeding
glorious: thou art clothed with majesty and honour.
Thou deckest thyself with light as it were
with a garment: and spreadest out the heavens
like a curtain.
Who layeth the beams of his chambers
in the waters: and maketh the clouds his
chariot, and walketh upon the wings of the wind.
He maketh his angels spirits: and his
ministers a flaming fire.
He laid the foundations of the earth: that
it never should move at any time.

He watereth the hills from above:
the earth is filled with the fruit of thy works.
He bringeth forth grass for the cattle:
and green herb for the service of men;
That he may bring food out of the earth,
and wine that maketh glad the heart of man:
and oil to make him a cheerful countenance,
and bread to strengthen man's heart.

O Lord, how manifold are thy works:
in wisdom hast thou made them all; the
earth is full of thy riches.
So is the great and wide sea also: wherein
are things creeping innumerable, both
small and great beasts.
There go the ships, and there is that
Leviathan: whom thou hast made to take
his pastime therein.

These wait all upon thee: that thou
mayest give them meat in due season.
When thou givest it them they gather it:
and when thou openest thy hand they are
filled with good.
When thou hidest thy face they are troubled:
when thou takest away their breath
they die, and are turned again to their dust.
When thou lettest thy breath go forth
they shall be made: and thou shalt renew
the face of the earth.
The glorious Majesty of the Lord shall
endure for ever: the Lord shall rejoice in his works.
The earth shall tremble at the look of him:
if he do but touch the hills, they shall smoke.
I will sing unto the Lord as long as I live:
I will praise my God while I have my being.

◆

The Russian writer Dostoevsky wrote:

Love all God's creation, both the whole and every grain of sand. Love
every leaf, every ray of light. Love the animals, love the plants, love
each separate thing. If thou love each thing then thou wilt perceive
the mystery of God in all; and when thou perceivest this, then thou
wilt thenceforward grow every day to a fuller understanding of it.

◆

The poet William Blake wrote this in his poem 'Auguries of Innocence':

To see a World in a Grain of Sand,
And a Heaven in a Wild Flower,
Hold Infinity in the palm of your hand,
And Eternity in an hour.

◆

The following was written by Henry Suso:

I place before my inward eyes myself with all that I am – my body, soul, and all my powers – and I gather round me all the creatures which God ever created in heaven, on earth, and in all the elements, each one severally with its name, whether birds of the air, beasts of the forest, fishes of the water, leaves and grass of the earth, or the innumerable sand of the sea, and to these I add all the little specks of dust which glance in the sunbeams, with all the little drops of water which ever fell or are falling from dew, snow, or rain, and I wish that each of these had a sweetly sounding stringed instrument, fashioned from my heart's inmost blood, striking on which they might each send up to our dear and gentle God a new and lofty strain of praise for ever and ever. And then the loving arms of my soul stretch out and extend themselves towards the innumerable multitude of all creatures, and my intention is, just as a free and blithesome leader of a choir stirs up the singers of his company, even so to turn them all to good account by inciting them to sing joyously, and to offer up their hearts to God.

Day 5

In this poem by Gerard Manley Hopkins, the poet wonders at the contrasts in God's creation, both in the natural world and in the world of man. He praises God for pattern and variety.

'Pied Beauty'
by Gerard Manley Hopkins

Glory be to God for dappled things –
For skies of couple-colour as a brinded cow;
For rose-moles all in stipple upon trout that swim;
Fresh-firecoal chestnut-falls; finches' wings;
Landscape plotted and pieced – fold, fallow, and plough;
And all trades, their gear and tackle and trim.

All things counter, original, spare, strange;
Whatever is fickle, freckled (who knows how?)
With swift, slow; sweet, sour; adazzle, dim;
He fathers-forth whose beauty is past change:
Praise him.

♦

This passage is about giving and receiving.

St Paul's Second Letter to the Corinthians, chapter 9, verses 6–15

Remember: sparse sowing, sparse reaping, sow bountifully, and you will reap bountifully. Each person should give as he has decided for himself; there should be no reluctance, no sense of compulsion; God loves a cheerful giver. And it is in God's power to provide you richly with every good gift; thus you will have ample means in yourselves to meet each and every situation, with enough and to spare for every good cause. Scripture says of such a man: 'He has lavished his gifts on the needy, his benevolence stands fast for ever.' Now he who provides seed for sowing and bread for food will provide the seed for you to sow; he will multiply it and swell the harvest of your benevolence, and you will always be rich enough to be generous. Through our action such generosity will issue in thanksgiving to God, for as a piece of willing service this is not only a contribution towards the needs of God's people; more than that, it overflows in a flood of thanksgiving to God. For through the proof which this affords, many will give honour to God when they see how humbly you obey him and how faithfully you confess the gospel of Christ; and will thank him for your liberal contribution to their need and to the general good. And as they join in prayer on your behalf, their hearts will go out to you because of the richness of the grace which God has imparted to you. Thanks be to God for his gift beyond words!

Day 6

These two passages are also about the wonders of God's creation, but they also touch upon the mess that human beings can make of it.

From The Far Side of the Street
by Bruce Hutchinson

Only an eye sated with too much print or too many electronic images is blind to the forest's infinitely varied colours. Only the ear dulled by the city's rumble is deaf to the forest's distinct utterance. Only the nose blunted by the city's fumes will not perceive the astringent whiff of conifer, the honeyed fragrance of blossom, the chaste scent of lichen. Only the hand numbed by soft living can fail to distinguish, even in darkness, the separate feel of the cedar's smooth webbing, the rough texture of the fir.

Any man of average intelligence will see that the forest has a sixth sense of its own. When countless millions of cells multiply by sure plan and long-tested architecture; when roots thinner than silk and strong as steel never cease their quest for moisture and hidden chemical; when pumps and capillary plumbing, which man has yet to invent or understand, carry the liquid upward to synthesize the tree's food by means unknown and exude the oxygen of all animal life; when trunk and limb swell and spread as if an engineer had designed them for stress and strain; when the forest, without eyes, unerringly finds the sun and burrows in the dark; when, mindless, it knows how to heal its wounds and rear its children; when, anchored to the earth, it marches generation by generation to recover its lost domain and expunge its human conqueror; when, indeed, the forest defies all laws and logic known to humans, then, perhaps man witnesses a kind of knowledge totally different from his own, a latent intelligence which, some day, he may learn to share. So far, he has only learnt how to destroy it.

♦

From The Seven Storey Mountain
by Thomas Merton

It is only the infinite mercy and love of God that has prevented us from tearing ourselves to pieces and destroying His entire creation long ago. People seem to think that it is in some way a proof that no merciful God exists, if we have so many wars. On the contrary, consider how in spite of centuries of sin and greed and lust and cruelty and hatred and avarice and oppression and injustice, spawned and bred by the free wills of men, the human race can still recover, each time, and can still produce men and women who overcome evil with good, hatred with love, greed with charity, lust and cruelty with sanctity. How could all this be possible without the merciful love of God, pouring out His grace upon us? Can there be any doubt where wars come from and where peace comes from, when the children of this world, excluding God from their peace conferences, only manage to bring about greater and greater wars the more they talk about peace?

We have only to open our eyes and look about us to see what our sins are doing to the world, and have done. But we cannot see.

There is not a flower that opens, not a seed that falls into the ground, and not an ear of wheat that nods on the end of its stalk in the wind that does not preach and proclaim the greatness and the mercy of God to the whole world.

There is not an act of kindness or generosity, not an act of sacrifice done, or a word of peace and gentleness spoken, not a child's prayer uttered, that does not sing hymns to God before His throne, and in the eyes of men, and before their faces.

How does it happen that in the thousands of generations of murderers since Cain, our dark bloodthirsty ancestor, that some of us can still be saints? The quietness and hiddenness and placidity of the truly good people in the world all proclaim the glory of God.

All these things, all creatures, every graceful movement, every ordered act of the human will, all are sent to us as prophets from God. But because of our stubbornness they come to us only to blind us further.

We refuse to hear the million different voices through which God speaks to us, and every refusal hardens us more and more against His grace – and yet He continues to speak to us: and we say He is without mercy!

'But the Lord dealeth patiently for your sake, not willing that any should perish, but that all should return to penance.'

Day 7

These passages are about gratitude, which can be a burden when it goes with a feeling of obligation. In both these readings, however, it is a matter of faith and joy.

St Luke's Gospel, chapter 17, verses 11–19

In the course of his journey to Jerusalem he was travelling through the borderlands of Samaria and Galilee. As he was entering a village he was met by ten men with leprosy. They stood some way off and called out to him, 'Jesus, Master, take pity on us.' When he saw them he said, 'Go and show yourselves to the priests'; and while they were on their way, they were made clean. One of them, finding himself cured, turned back praising God aloud. He threw himself down at Jesus's feet and thanked him. And he was a Samaritan. At this Jesus said: 'Were not all ten cleansed? The other nine, where are they? Could none be found to come back and give praise to God except this foreigner?' And he said to the man, 'Stand up and go on your way; your faith has cured you.'

◆

From 'Gratefulness'
by George Herbert

Thou that hast giv'n so much to me,
Give one thing more, a grateful heart.
See how thy beggar works on thee
By art.
He makes thy gifts occasion more,
And says, If he in this be crossed,
All thou hast giv'n him heretofore
Is lost.
Wherefore I cry, and cry again;
And in no quiet canst thou be,
Till I a thankful heart obtain
Of thee:
Not thankful, when it pleaseth me;
As if thy blessings had spare days:
But such a heart, whose pulse may be
Thy praise.

12

Saints and saintly people

The theme of these readings is Saints, who have been called 'the athletes of God, the heroes and heroines of the Faith'.

Day 1

Thomas Merton, in describing the effect of God's love upon the human soul, also defines what it is to be a saint:

From The Seven Storey Mountain
by Thomas Merton

When a ray of light strikes a crystal, it gives a new quality to the crystal. And when God's infinitely disinterested love plays upon a human soul, the same kind of thing takes place. And that is the life called sanctifying grace.

The soul of man, left to its own natural level, is a potentially lucid crystal left in darkness. It is perfect in its own nature, but it lacks something that it can only receive from outside and above itself. But when the light shines in it, it becomes in a manner transformed into light and seems to lose its nature in the splendour of a higher nature, the nature of the light that is in it.

So the natural goodness of man, his capacity for love which must always be in some sense selfish if it remains in the natural order, becomes transfigured and transformed when the Love of God shines in it. What happens when a man loses himself completely in the Divine Life within him? This perfection is only for those who are called the saints – for those rather who *are* the saints and who live in the light of God alone.

Day 2

Christ's actions and words in St Matthew's Gospel inspired the life and work of St Francis of Assisi.

St Matthew's Gospel, chapter 8, verses 1–4, and chapter 25, verses 31–41

After he had come down from the hill he was followed by a great crowd. And now a leper approached him, bowed low, and said, 'Sir, if only you will, you can cleanse me.' Jesus stretched out his hand, touched him, and said, 'Indeed I will; be clean again.' And his leprosy was cured immediately. Then Jesus said to him, 'Be sure you tell nobody; but go and show yourself to the priest, and make the offering laid down by Moses for your cleansing; that will certify the cure.'

'When the Son of Man comes in his glory and all the angels with him, he will sit in state on his throne, with all the nations gathered before him. He will separate men into two groups, as a shepherd separates the sheep from the goats, and he will place the sheep on his right hand and the goats on his left. Then the king will say to those on his right hand, "You have my Father's blessing; come, enter and possess the kingdom that has been ready for you since the world was made. For when I was hungry, you gave me food; when thirsty, you gave me drink; when I was a stranger you took me into your home, when naked you clothed me; when I was ill you came to my help, when in prison you visited me." Then the righteous will reply, "Lord, when was it that we saw you hungry and fed you, or thirsty and gave you drink, a stranger and took you home, or naked and clothed you? When did we see you ill or in prison, and come to visit you?" And the king will answer, "I tell you this: anything you did for one of my brothers here, however humble, you did for me."'

♦

This is one author's description of the story of St Francis and the leper.

From Acts of Worship for Assemblies
by R H Lloyd

One of the most popular and loved of our saints is Francis of Assisi who lived between 1182 and 1226. He was the son of a wealthy wool merchant. As a youth he led a carefree life joining in the activities of his pleasure loving companions, and helping to organize feasts and banquets and taking part in jousts and ceremonial processions. His father encouraged Francis in these pursuits and kept him generously supplied with large sums of money, so that he became known throughout the region as a big spender. And then, quite suddenly, to everyone's astonishment, he turned his back on all this, and embraced a life of poverty which eventually led him to sainthood.

According to one account, the great turning point came as the result of an encounter with a leper. It is said that Francis was riding home after a riotous all-night party. As he approached Assisi, he saw a leper limping painfully towards him. The very sight of leprosy filled Francis with fear and loathing. As he drew abreast of the leper, he reined in his horse to the opposite side of the road and looked away. And then, on an impulse, he glanced at the leper and saw the ravaged face, the clawed hands and filthy rags. But, instead of experiencing a feeling of revulsion, he was swept with compassion. He dismounted and crossed over to the cowering figure and embraced him. Francis had never experienced such love! He took off his robe and put it on the leper, he emptied his pockets and handed over his money.

Returning to his horse, he remounted and continued on his way. Turning in his saddle, he raised his arm to wave goodbye, but was amazed to find no one there. The road, as far as the eye could see, was deserted. In that moment Francis realized that he had in fact embraced Jesus Christ.

Day 3

There are great martyrs whose deaths are an inspiration to the whole world; but there are also many insignificant people who have this courage. Such a one is Alyosha, a character in a novel by Solzhenitsyn, who is based on a real person whom the author knew during his imprisonment in a Soviet labour camp in Siberia.

From One Day in the Life of Ivan Denisovitch
by Alexander Solzhenitsyn

He must make his bed now – there wasn't much to it. Strip his mattress of the grubby blanket and lie on it (it must have been '41 when he last slept in sheets – that was at home).

Head on the pillow, stuffed with shavings of wood: feet in jacket sleeve; coat on top of blanket and – Glory be to Thee, O Lord. Another day over. Thank you I'm not spending tonight in the cells. Here it's still bearable.

He lay head to the window, but Alyosha, who slept next to him on the same level, across a low wooden railing, lay the opposite way, to catch the light. He was reading his Bible again.

The electric light was quite near. You could read and even sew by it.

Alyosha heard Shukhov's whispered prayer, and turning to him:

'There you are, Ivan Denisovich, your soul is begging to pray. Why, then, don't you give it its freedom?'

Shukhov stole a look at him. Alyosha's eyes glowed like two candles.

'Well Alyosha,' he said with a sigh, 'it's this way. Prayers are like those appeals of ours. Either they don't get through or they're returned with "rejected" scrawled across 'em.'

'But Ivan Denisovich, it's because you pray too rarely, and badly at that. Without really trying. That's why your prayers stay unanswered. One must never stop praying. If you have real faith you tell a mountain to move and it will move...'

Shukhov grinned and rolled another cigarette. He took a light from the Estonian.

'Don't talk bunkum, Alyosha. I've never seen a mountain move.

Well, to tell the truth, I've never seen a mountain at all. But you, now, you prayed in the Caucasus with all that Baptist club of yours – did you make a single mountain move?'

They were a luckless lot too. What harm did they do anyone by praying to God? Every man Jack of 'em given twenty-five years.

'Oh, we didn't pray for that, Ivan Denisovich,' Alyosha said earnestly. Bible in hand, he drew nearer to Shukhov till they lay face to face. 'Of all earthly and mortal things Our Lord commanded us to pray only for our daily bread. "Give us this day our daily bread." '

'Our ration, you mean?' asked Shukhov.

But Alyosha didn't give up. Arguing more with his eyes than his tongue, he plucked at Shukhov's sleeve, stroked his arm, and said:

'Ivan Denisovich, you shouldn't pray to get parcels or for extra skilly, not for that. Things that man puts a high price on are vile in the eyes of Our Lord. We must pray about things of the spirit – that the Lord Jesus should remove the scum of anger from our hearts...'

'Well,' he said conclusively, 'however much you pray it doesn't shorten your stretch. You'll sit it out from beginning to end anyhow.'

'Oh, you mustn't pray for that either,' said Alyosha, horrified. 'Why d'you want freedom? In freedom your last grain of faith will be choked with weeds. You should rejoice that you're in prison. Here you have time to think about your soul. As the Apostle Paul wrote: "Why all these tears? Why are you trying to weaken my resolution? For my part I am ready not merely to be bound but even to die for the name of the Lord Jesus." ' Alyosha was speaking the truth. His voice and his eyes left no doubt that he was happy in prison.

Day 4

Nowadays we regard slavery with abhorrence. It is difficult for us to realize that for most of human history, some people have belonged to others like domesticated animals. One of the great heroes who perceived the gross injustice of this was William Wilberforce.
This is an article about him.

'Saint who loved one-liners'
by The Right Reverend Richard Harries, Bishop of Oxford

The Church of England keeps July 29 as a memorial to William Wilberforce, who died on that date in 1833. He was born with many advantages. His family became rich from trade to the Baltic. He was a born orator. 'Of all the men I know,' said his friend Pitt, 'Wilberforce has the greatest natural eloquence.'

Above all, he had charm. People spoke of his vivacity, his delight in little things. 'I have always heard', said the French writer Madame de Staël, 'that he was the most religious, but now I find he is the wittiest, man in England.' Wilberforce once told a missionary meeting that he had had a dream that he was in hell. 'It was just like here,' he added, almost to himself. 'I could not get near the fire for parsons.'

Wilberforce had a love of pleasure and with his abilities could have done almost anything he wanted with his life. He was converted to a more serious and personal understanding of Christianity and, instead of a life of pleasure, he chose public service; instead of great office, he chose a great cause. He gave his life, first to the abolition of the slave traffic and then to the abolition of slavery in the British empire. The vested interests were large, the opposition formidable, but three days before he died word came that his life's work had succeeded.

Inevitably, during this century Wilberforce's reputation has fluctuated. Historians have accused him of supporting liberal causes abroad and opposing them at home; they have pointed to economic rather than moral factors as the determining cause in the abolition of slavery.

Yet as a biographer, Ian Bradley, has written: 'It is still the saintliness of Wilberforce that shines out... a life full of fun and gaiety and never over-pious or sanctimonious.' There is still enough goodness in his character to think of him, as his contemporaries did, as 'The Saint'.

Wilberforce challenges a number of modern stereotypes. He shows that evangelical spirituality, far from being cold or austere, can be warm and winning. Second, he shows that evangelicals are not committed to the political status quo.

Third, he shows that the personal and the political, far from being in opposition, need to be held together in the Christian life. Wilberforce knew that his intense personal conviction also needed political expression. Slavery was an affront to human beings made in the image of God and for whom Christ had died.

So it is in the modern world. From time to time the Church will inescapably, with a profound moral passion, be drawn into the realm of politics. Sometimes, on some issues, this will be the only way of being true to the Gospel and a sincere follower of Jesus Christ.

Day 5

This reading is about Leo Tolstoy, the great Russian novelist.

From How Can We Know?
by A N Wilson

Here was the greatest genius who had ever written a novel. He was a Russian aristocrat, an ex-soldier, a sensualist, one of the richest characters (in all senses of those words) in the history of literature. And yet, at the very summit of his fame, he wanted to renounce everything, to abandon his estates, his money, the practice of literature, the exercise of his carnal appetites, and to live a life of poverty, like the peasants on his estates. And why? Because he had become convinced that the Sermon preached by Jesus on the mountain towards the beginning of St Matthew's Gospel was simply and literally true.

◆

This is what Tolstoy wrote about what Jesus said in the Sermon on the Mount when he urged people to love their enemies.

But not only do I now know that my separation from other nations is an evil, ruining my welfare, but I also know the temptation that led me into that evil, and I can no longer, as I did formerly, consciously and quietly serve it. I know that that temptation lies in the delusion that my welfare is bound up only with that of the people of my own nation, and not with that of all the peoples of the earth. I now know that my union with other people cannot be severed by a line of frontier and by Government decrees about my belonging to this or that nation. I now know that all men everywhere are equals and brothers. Remembering now all the evil I have done, suffered, and seen, resulting from the enmity of nations, it is clear to me that the cause of it all lay in the gross fraud called patriotism and love of one's country. Remembering my education, I now see that a feeling of hostility to other nations, a feeling of separation from them, was never really natural to me, but that all these evil feelings were artificially inoculated into me by an insane education. I now understand the meaning of the words: Do good to your enemies; behave to them as to your own people. You are all children of one Father; so be like your Father, i.e. do not make distinctions between your own people and other peoples; be the same with them all. I now understand that my welfare is only possible if I acknowledge my unity with all the people of the world without exception. I believe this. And that belief has changed my whole valuation of what is good and evil, lofty and mean. What seemed to me good and lofty – love of the fatherland, of one's own people, of one's State, and service of it to the detriment of the welfare of other peoples, the military achievements of men, all this now appears to me repulsive and pitiable. What seemed to me bad and shameful – rejection of fatherland, and cosmopolitanism – now appears to me, on the contrary, good and noble.

Day 6

In St Mark's Gospel, Jesus tells the people what they must do to become true Christians.

St Mark's Gospel, chapter 8, verses 34–38

Then he called the people to him, as well as his disciples, and said to them, 'Anyone who wishes to be a follower of mine must leave self behind; he must take up his cross, and come with me. Whoever cares for his own safety is lost; but if a man will let himself be lost for my sake and for the Gospel, that man is safe. What does a man gain by winning the whole world at the cost of his true self? What can he give to buy that self back?

◆

Now we look at the ideas of a man who followed this teaching. He is called Albert Schweitzer and he died in 1965. He was a successful scholar and musician who trained as a doctor and went to a remote part of West Africa where he established a hospital to help people who had no medical care at all. The basis of his belief was what he called 'reverence for life'. This is how he describes it:

Ethics is nothing else than reverence for life. Reverence for life affords me my fundamental principle of morality, namely, that good consists in maintaining, assisting and enhancing life, and that to destroy, to harm or to hinder life is evil.

Although the phrase 'reverence for life' may perhaps sound a trifle unreal, yet that which it denotes is something which never lets go its hold of the man in whose thought it has once found a place. Sympathy, love, and, in general, all enthusiastic feelings of real value are summed up in it.

Reverence for life does not allow me to appropriate my own happiness. At moments when I should like to enjoy myself without a care, it brings before me thoughts of the misery I have seen and surmised. It refuses to allow me to banish my uneasiness. Just as the wave has no existence of its own, but it is part of the continual movement of the ocean, thus I also am destined never to experience my life as self-contained, but always as part of the experience which is going on around me. An uncomfortable doctrine prompts me in whispered words. You are happy, it says. Therefore you are called to give up much. Whatever you have received more than others in health, in talents, in ability, in success, in a pleasant childhood, in harmonious conditions of home life, all this you must not take to yourself as a matter of course. You must pay a price for it. You must render in return an unusually great sacrifice of your life for other life. The voice of the true ethic is dangerous for the happy when they have the courage to listen to it. For them there is no quenching of the irrational fire which glows in it. It challenges them in an attempt to lead them away from the natural road, and to see whether it can make them the adventurers of self-sacrifice, of whom the world has too few.

Day 7

This is a leaflet issued by Dr Martin Luther King, who worked, and eventually died, for the rights of black people in the Southern States of the USA. In December 1956 he achieved his first major victory when the Supreme Court in the United States declared that it was illegal to have separate sections in buses for blacks and whites. He issued this leaflet to his congregation, who faced the difficult task of travelling for the first time on buses with white people. His advice, however, could equally apply to anyone who is persecuted on public transport for whatever reason.

'Integrated Bus Suggestions'

Dec. 19, 1956 – This is a historic week because segregation on buses has now been declared unconstitutional. Within a few days the Supreme Court Mandate will reach Montgomery and you will be re-boarding integrated buses. This places upon us all a tremendous responsibility of maintaining, in the face of what could be some unpleasantness, a calm and loving dignity befitting good citizens and members of our race. If there is violence in word or deed it must not be our people who commit it.

For your help and convenience the following suggestions are made. Will you read, study and memorize them so that our nonviolent determination may not be endangered. First, some general suggestions:

1 Not all white people are opposed to integrated buses. Accept goodwill on the part of many.
2 The whole bus is now for the use of *all* people. Take a vacant seat.
3 Pray for guidance and commit yourself to complete non-violence in word and action as you enter the bus.
4 Demonstrate the calm dignity of our Montgomery people in your actions.
5 In all things observe ordinary rules of courtesy and good behaviour.
6 Remember that this is not a victory for Negroes alone, but for all Montgomery and the South. Do not boast! Do not brag!
7 Be quiet but friendly; proud, but not arrogant; joyous, but not boisterous.
8 Be loving enough to absorb evil and understanding enough to turn an enemy into a friend.

Now for some specific suggestions:

1 The bus driver is in charge of the bus and has been instructed to obey the law. Assume that he will co-operate in helping you occupy any vacant seat.
2 Do not deliberately sit by a white person, unless there is no other seat.
3 In sitting down by a person, white or coloured, say 'May I' or 'Pardon me,' as you sit. This is a common courtesy.
4 If cursed, do not curse back. If pushed, do not push back. If struck, do not strike back, but evidence love and goodwill at all times.
5 In case of an incident, talk as little as possible, and always in a quiet tone. Do not get up from your seat! Report all serious incidents to the bus driver.
6 For the first few days try to get on the bus with a friend in whose non-violence you have confidence. You can uphold one another by a glance or a prayer.

7 If another person is being molested, do not arise to go to his defense, but pray for the oppressor and use moral and spiritual force to carry on the struggle for justice.

8 According to your own ability and personality, do not be afraid to experiment with new and creative techniques for achieving reconciliation and social change.

9 If you feel you cannot take it, walk for another week or two. We have confidence in our people. GOD BLESS YOU ALL.

Day 8

These extracts are about the work of a saintly woman who is still alive. She is Mother Teresa. The central belief and theme of her life is expressed in the New Testament.

First Letter of St John, chapter 4, verses 7–21

Dear friends, let us love one another, because love is from God. Everyone who loves is a child of God and knows God, but the unloving know nothing of God. For God is love; and his love was disclosed to us in this, that he sent his only Son into the world to bring us life. The love I speak of is not our love for God, but the love he showed to us in sending his Son as the remedy for the defilement of our sins. If God thus loved us, dear friends, we in turn are bound to love one another. Though God has never been seen by any man, God himself dwells in us if we love one another; his love is brought to perfection within us.

Here is the proof that we dwell in him and he dwells in us: he has imparted his Spirit to us. Moreover, we have seen for ourselves, and we attest that the Father sent the Son to be the saviour of the world, and if a man acknowledges that Jesus is the Son of God, God dwells in him and he dwells in God. Thus we have come to know and believe the love which God has for us.

God is love; he who dwells in love is dwelling in God, and God in him. This is for us the perfection of love, to have confidence on the day of judgement, and this we can have, because even in this world we are as he is.

There is no room for fear in love; perfect love banishes fear. Fo fear brings with it the pains of judgement; and anyone who is afraic has not attained to love in its perfection. We love because he lovec us first. But if a man says, 'I love God', while hating his brother, he is a liar. If he does not love the brother whom he has seen, it can not be that he loves God whom he has not seen. And indeed this command comes to us from Christ himself: that he who loves Goc must also love his brother.

♦

Here is a passage about Mother Teresa.

From Something Beautiful for God
by Malcolm Muggeridge

I called to mind a particular incident which had greatly affected me at the time, to the point that it sometimes came into my dreams. was being driven one evening in my car when my driver knockec someone over – something as easily done then as now, with the crowded pavements spilling over into the roadway. With great re sourcefulness, and knowing the brawls that could so easily develop when a European car was involved in a street accident, my drive jumped out, grabbed the injured man, put him in the driving sea beside him, and drove away at top speed to the nearest hospital There, I rather self-righteously insisted on seeing that the man wa. properly attended to (as it turned out, he was not seriously hurt) and, being a Sahib, was able to follow him into the emergency ward It was a scene of inconceivable confusion and horror, with patient stretched out on the floor, in the corridors, everywhere. While I wa waiting, a man was brought in who had just cut his throat from ea to ear. It was too much; I made off, back to my comfortable flat and a stiff whisky and soda, to expatiate through the years to come on Bengal's wretched social conditions, and what a scandal it was, anc how it was greatly to be hoped that the competent authorities would… and so on.

I ran away and stayed away; Mother Teresa moved in and stayed That was the difference. She, a nun, rather slightly built, with a few rupees in her pocket; not particularly clever, or particularly gifted in the arts of persuasion. Just with this Christian love shining about her in her heart and on her lips. Just prepared to follow her Lord, and in accordance with his instructions regard every derelict left to die in the streets as him; to hear in the cry of every abandoned child, even in the tiny squeak of the discarded foetus, the cry of the Bethlehem child; to recognize in every leper's stumps the hands which once touched sightless eyes and made them see, rested on distracted heads and made them calm, brought back health to sick flesh and twisted limbs...

What the poor need, Mother Teresa is fond of saying, even more than food and clothing and shelter (though they need these, too, desperately), is to be wanted. It is the outcast state their poverty imposes upon them that is the most agonizing. She has a place in her heart for them all. To her, they are all children of God, for whom Christ died, and so deserving of all love. If God counts the hairs of each of their heads, if none are excluded from the salvation the Crucifixion offers, who will venture to exclude them from earthly blessings and esteem; pronounce this life unnecessary, that one better terminated or never begun? I never experienced so perfect a sense of human equality as with Mother Teresa among her poor. Her love for them, reflecting God's love, makes them equal, as brothers and sisters within a family are equal, however widely they differ in intellectual and other attainments, in physical beauty and grace.

This is the only equality there is on earth, and it cannot be embodied in laws, enforced by coercion, or promoted by protest and upheaval, deriving, as it does, from God's love, which, like the rain from heaven, falls on the just and the unjust, on rich and poor, alike.

Appendix 1: Prayers

◆

The following prayers, which have been chosen for the appropriate beauty of their words, may be used with the readings in assemblies. Suggestions are given for which days they are most suitable.

Appropriate for: Section 1, Day 2; Section 2, Day 10; Section 3, Day 3; Section 5, Day 6; Section 8, Day 8; Section 12, Day 2.

Lord, make us instruments of thy peace.
Where there is hatred, let us sow love;
Where there is injury, pardon;
Where there is discord, union;
Where there is doubt, faith;
Where there is despair, hope;
Where there is darkness, light;
Where there is sadness, joy;

Appropriate for: Section 4, Day 5; Section 6, Day 7; Section 7, Day 1; Section 9, Day 10; Section 10, Day 6; Section 12, Day 7.

O Divine Master, grant that we may
not so much seek to be consoled as to console;
to be understood as to understand;
to be loved as to love;
through the love of thy Son who died for us,
Jesus Christ our Lord. Amen

(St Francis of Assisi, 1182–1226)

Appropriate for: Section 1, Day 1; Section 2, Day 1 & Day 9; Section 5, Day 1 & Day 8; Section 8, Day 9; Section 9, Day 11; Section 12, Day 1.

Teach us, good Lord
To serve thee as thou deservest;
To give and not to count the cost;
To fight and not to heed the wounds;
To toil and not to seek for rest;
To labour and not to ask for any reward,
Save that of knowing that we do thy will. Amen

(Ignatius Loyola, 1491–1556)

Appropriate for: Section 2, Day 11; Section 4, Day 6; Section 8, Day 1; Section 9, Day 4; Section 10, Day 1; Section 11, Day 3.

O Holy Spirit, giver of light and life,
Impart to us thoughts higher than our own thoughts
and prayers better than our own prayers,
and powers beyond our own powers,
that we may spend and be spent
in the ways of love and goodness,
after the perfect image
of our Lord and Saviour Jesus Christ. Amen

Appropriate for: Section 3, Day 4; Section 7, Day 6; Section 9, Day 1 & Day 9; Section 10, Day 7; Section 11, Day 5; Section 12, Day 8.

O Lord Jesus Christ, who hast taught us that it is more blessed to give than to receive, and that to whom much is given much shall be required: Pour into our hearts the spirit of thine own abundant generosity, and make us ready and eager to share with others what we ourselves have so richly and freely received. Amen   (R H Lloyd)

Appropriate for: Section 5, Day 5; Section 7, Day 3; Section 9, Day 5; Section 12, Day 5.

Lord, you have taught us
that all our doings without love are nothing worth.
Send your Holy Spirit
and pour into our hearts that most excellent gift of love,
the true bond of peace and of all virtues,
without which whoever lives is counted dead before you.
Grant this for the sake of your only Son, Jesus Christ our Lord.
                    (from *The Book of Common Prayer*)

Appropriate for: Section 8, Day 6; Section 9, Day 9

Set a watch, O Lord, upon our tongue,
that we may never speak the cruel word which is untrue;
or, being true, is not the whole truth;
or, being wholly true, is merciless;
for the love of Jesus Christ our Lord. Amen.

Appropriate for: Section 1, Day 3; Section 2, Day 3 & Day 5; Section 4, Day 2; Section 7, Day 2; Section 8, Day 4; Section 9, Day 6.

Take from us, O God,
All pride and vanity,
All boasting and forwardness;
And give us the true courage that
shows itself by gentleness,
The true wisdom that shows itself by simplicity,
And the true power that shows itself by modesty;
through Jesus Christ our Lord. Amen

(Charles Kingsley, 1819–1875)

Appropriate for: Section 2, Day 2; Section 3, Day 1; Section 5, Day 7 Section 8, Day 9; Section 10, Day 3; Section 11, Day 2; Section 12 Day 3.

Almighty God,
to whom all hearts are open,
all desires known,
and from whom no secrets are hidden:
cleanse the thoughts of our hearts
by the inspiration of your Holy Spirit,
that we may perfectly love you,
and worthily magnify your holy name;
through Christ our Lord. Amen

(from *The Book of Common Prayer*)

Appropriate for: Section 3, Day 2 & Day 6; Section 6, Day 2; Section 8, Day 5; Section 9, Day 3.

O Lord in whose hands are life and death, by whose power we are sustained, forgive us that we have suffered the days and hours, of which we must give account, to pass away without any endeavour to accomplish thy will. Make us to remember, O God, that every day is thy gift and ought to be used according to thy command. Grant us therefore so to repent of our negligence that we may pass the time which thou shalt yet allow us in diligent service; through Jesus Christ.

(Samuel Johnson, 1709–1784)

Appropriate for: Section 3, Day 5; Section 6, Day 4; Section 11, Day 1; Section 12, Day 4.

O God, who hast ordained that whatever is to be desired should be sought by labour, and who, by thy blessing, bringest honest labour to good effect: look with mercy upon our studies and endeavours. Grant us, O Lord, to design only what is lawful and right, and afford us calmness of mind and steadiness of purpose, that we may so do thy will in this short life as to obtain happiness in the world to come.

(Samuel Johnson, 1709–1784)

Appropriate for: Section 2, Day 7; Section 3, Day 7; Section 4, Day 4; Section 6, Day 3; Section 9, Day 7; Section 11, Day 6.

Almighty God, our heavenly Father,
we have sinned against thee,
through our own fault,
in thought, and word, and deed,
and in what we have left undone.
For thy Son our Lord Jesus Christ's sake,
forgive us all that is past;
and grant that we may serve thee,
in newness of life,
to the glory of thy name.

(an Order for Holy Communion)

Appropriate for: Section 6, Day 5; Section 7, Day 4; Section 8, Day 3; Section 10, Day 5.

O Lord, support us all the day long of this troublous life, until the shades lengthen and the evening comes, the busy world is hushed, the fever of life over, and our work done; then Lord in thy mercy grant us safe lodging, a holy rest and peace at the last; through Jesus Christ our Lord.

(Cardinal Newman, 1801–1890)

Appropriate for: Section 2, Day 4; Section 5, Day 4; Section 6, Day 6; Section 7, Day 5; Section 9, Day 12; Section 12, Day 6.

Almighty God, give us grace that we may cast away the works of darkness, and put upon us the armour of light, now in the time of this mortal life, in which thy Son Jesus Christ came to visit us in great humility; that in the last day when he shall come again in his glorious majesty to judge both the quick and the dead, we may rise to the life immortal, through him who liveth and reigneth with thee and the Holy Ghost, now and ever.

(from *The Book of Common Prayer*)

Appropriate for: Section 1, Day 5; Section 2, Day 8; Section 8, Day 7; Section 10, Day 2.

> Suffer us not to mock ourselves with falsehood
> Teach us to care and not to care
> Teach us to sit still
> Even among these rocks,
> Our peace in His will
> And even among these rocks
> Sister, mother
> And spirit of the river, spirit of the sea,
> Suffer me not to be separated
> And let my cry come unto Thee.

(from 'Ash Wednesday' by T S Eliot)

Appropriate for: Section 1, Day 2; Section 2, Day 6; Section 5, Day 3; Section 6, Day 1; Section 10, Day 4; Section 11, Day 4 & Day 7.

Almighty God, Father of all mercies, we thine unworthy servants do give thee most humble and hearty thanks for all thy goodness and loving-kindness to us and to all men;

We bless thee for our creation, preservation, and all the blessings of this life; but above all for thine inestimable love in the redemption of the world by our Lord Jesus Christ, for the means of grace, and for the hope of glory. And we beseech thee, give us that due sense of all thy mercies, that our hearts may be unfeignedly thankful, and that we shew forth thy praise, not only with our lips, but in our lives; by giving up ourselves to thy service, and by walking before thee in holiness and righteousness all our days; through Jesus Christ our Lord, to whom with thee and the Holy Ghost be all honour and glory, world without end. Amen.

(from *The Book of Common Prayer*)

Appendix 2: Passages used in this book

◆

Abbreviations
NEB – The New English Bible
RSV – The Revised Standard Version
NJB – The New Jerusalem Bible
AV – The Authorised Version (1611)
JBP – The New Testament in Modern English translated by
    J B Phillips

1 Readings for Christmas

5 The story of Saint Peter

9 *The Ten Commandments*

Appendix 3: List of authors

◆

AESOP: 'The Body and Its Members'; 'The Wind and the Sun'

AQUINAS, St Thomas

AUSTEN, Jane: *Sense and Sensibility*

BETJEMAN, John: 'Christmas'; 'The Conversion of St Paul'

BLAKE, William: 'Auguries of Innocence'

BUNYAN, John: *The Pilgrim's Progress*

CASSIDY, Sheila: *Good Friday People*

CHESTERTON, G K: *Orthodoxy*; 'The Donkey'

CRANE, Stephen: 'The Voice of God'

DAVIDMAN, Joy: *Smoke on the Mountain*

DONNE, John: *Meditation*

DOSTOEVSKY, Fedor: *The Brothers Karamazov*

ELIOT, T S: 'The Rock'; 'The Cultivation of Christmas Trees'; 'The Journey of the Magi'; Ash Wednesday

GOLLANCZ, Victor: *A Year of Grace*

GRAHAME, Kenneth: *The Wind in the Willows*

GRENFELL, Joyce: *By Herself and Her Friends*

GRYN, Rabbi: his experiences in Auschwitz

HAILSHAM, Lord: *The Door Wherein I Went*

HARCOURT, Pierre d': *The Real Enemy Is Within*

HARRIES, The Right Reverend Bishop Richard: 'Saint who loved one liners'

HERBERT, George: 'Love'; 'Gratefulness'

HOPKINS, Gerard Manley: 'Pied Beauty'

HUTCHINSON, Bruce: *The Far Side of the Street*

INNES, Mary: *Metamorphosis of Ovid*

JENNINGS, Elizabeth: 'Afterthought'

JOHNSON, Samuel: Prayers

KEMPIS, Thomas à: Prayer

KENDON Frank: 'The Merchant's Carol'

KING, Martin Luther: 'Integrated Bus Suggestions'

KINGSLEY, Charles: Prayer

KIPLING, Rudyard: *Kim*

LEWIS, C S: *The Lion, The Witch and the Wardrobe*

LLOYD, R H: The Russian Prince, The Tumbler and St Francis

OYOLA, Ignatius: Prayer

1ACNEICE, Louis: 'Prayer before Birth'

1ERTON, Thomas: *The Seven Storey Mountain*

1ILLER, Daniel: Extract from F C Scott memorial lecture

1UGGERIDGE, Malcolm: *Something Beautiful for God*

JEWMAN, Cardinal: Prayer

ÉGUY, Charles: *Basic Verities*

LATH, Sylvia: *Letters Home*

LATO: 'Georgias'

REZZOLINI, Guiseppe: article in *La Voce* 1911.

)UOIST, Michel: *Prayers of Life*

EID, Forrest: 'Apostate'

OSSETTI, Christina: 'Easter Monday'

CHWEITZER, Albert: 'Ethics'

COTT HOLLAND, Canon Henry: 'The Next Room'

OLZHENITSYN, Alexander: *One Day in the Life of Ivan Denisovich*

OUTHWELL, Robert: 'New Prince, New Pomp'; ' The Burning Babe'

TEPHENS, James: 'A Singing in the Air'

USO, Heinrich: *The Life of Blessed Henry Suso*

ERESA, Mother: *A Gift for God*

ERESA, St of Àvila

HOMPSON, Francis: 'The Kingdom of God'

OLSTOY, Leo: *Resurrection*; *What I Believe*

OWNSEND G F: comment on Aesop's fable

RAHERNE, Thomas: *Centuries of Meditation*

URGENEV, Ivan: *Dream Tales and Prose Poems*

VEIL, Simone: *Selected Essays and Seventy Letters*

VELLS, H G: *The Outline of History*

VILSON, A N: *How Can We Know?*

VORDSWORTH, William: extract from 'Lines composed a few miles
above Tintern Abbey'

EVTUSHENKO, Yevgeny: *A Precocious Autobiography*

Index